Reviews by Cat Ellington

Books by Cat Ellington

Reviews by Cat Ellington
The Complete Anthology, Vol. 2

Cat Ellington

Quill Pen Ink Publishing

THE BEAUTY OF EXPRESSION™

CHICAGO

PAPERBACK ISBN: 978-0-692-18534-6
HARDCOVER ISBN: 978-1-7370971-6-7

Library of Congress Control Number: 2022362728

Cover design: Hues of the Reviews
Vol. 2 Hue: Robin's Egg
The Cat Ellington Literary Collection

Published by Quill Pen Ink Publishing
Chicago, Illinois, USA
https://quill-pen-ink-publishing.business.site/

Quill Pen Ink Publishing, 2018

Hardcover Edition: October 2021

Printed in the U.S.A.

Dedication

To Butch and Otis—
The baddest Marines in the Earth realm

Preface

We're back, my dearest men and women – this time with book 2 in the Reviews by Cat Ellington series. I hope that you all enjoyed reading Reviews by Cat Ellington: The Complete Anthology, Vol. 1, which laid the foundation for this ongoing series devoted to my passion for books, reading them, and reviewing them through the many years.

My library is 1,600+ titles and growing! Whew! Can any man or woman read *that* many books in his or her lifetime? It's possible, it's possible, but it would be quite a challenge. Because having that many books accounts for a great deal of reading. So, what is my best method for going about it all? One book at a time, of course, one book at a time. One love.

My dearest men and women, especially those of you who are my contemporary bibliophiles, you will all join me on this new adventure, being Reviews by Cat Ellington: The Complete Anthology, Vol. 2, yes? Oh, it's going to be so exciting having you all along for the ride! So sit back and relax. I'll handle the wheel.
Y'all enjoy yourselves now, y'hear?

Acknowledgments

First and foremost, it is my kind pleasure to ascribe the grandest of glory to my Heavenly Father, the Most-High God, and to my Lord and Holy Savior Christ Jesus, as well as to the glorious Holy Spirit. Three humbled cheers for the tremendously beloved Holy Trinity from whom all great blessings flow. Amen. Amen. And Amen one more time.

Joe, you mean the world to me. And I love you. Thank you for your love, patience, and support.

Nathaniel, Nairobi, and Naras, when I hear the three of you say to me that, 'We love our mama,' well, it just gets right here. I love y'all, too, babies. And I wouldn't trade either one of you for anything.

Mama, understanding comes with life experience. And having my offspring now makes me appreciate you and your parenting that much more. I am honored to be your daughter, and I love you.

Freddie and Maurice, I love you both. Thank you for your courageous faith over the years. My respect and admiration will forever be at your joint command.

I extend a special thank you to David Wogahn, publisher of *The Book Reviewer Yellow Pages*, and to Maree Paras, the woman by way of whom I received my first listing in the 8th edition of the Pages. To this day, I am still grateful, humble, and undeniably honored to feature, even consecutively, in *The Book Reviewer Yellow Pages*. For literary criticism is, much like music, one of my few undying passions.

Thank you to Jessica Zillhart of the Saint Paul Public Library. To you, I am eternally grateful.

Thank you to Cara Eakes and the entire staff at BiblioBoard. I appreciate all of you.

Thank you to Becky Robinson and Kristin Elliott of Hometown Reads. On behalf of Quill Pen Ink Publishing, I extend our deepest gratitude.

Thank you to Vinny O'Hara, Christine Liston, Jennifer, and the entire editorial staff in the Author Ad Network and BookGoodies Networks. I appreciate all of your hard work on behalf of the literary community. And I will cherish you always.

And a very special thank you to Ms. Kim Somers, of Kim Somers Voice Overs, for her exquisite narration of Reviews by Cat Ellington: The Complete Anthology, Vol. 1. I will forever appreciate you, Kim. Your voice is truly heavenly.

Table of Contents

Chapter 1

The Writer Continues Her Journey

Cat Ellington's review of Another Country by James Baldwin

My rating: 5 of 5 stars

Date read: March, 1996

"You can determine the caliber of a man by the amount of opposition it takes to discourage him."
—Rocky Balboa

That legendary quote comes to mind when I estimate the vitriolic James Baldwin masterwork currently under examination, said work of legend titled *Another Country*.

Set in 1950s America, this Baldwin classic conquers every aspect of an American society traveling along the path of self-destruction. Part iron and part clay, America is a nation in peril, a divided universe rotating around a bitter-spirited oppressor who cannot obtain a moment's rest unless—or until—he or she has broken the spirit of the oppressed. Exposing the workings of evil operating in those who have pledged allegiance to the flag of White superiority, the great Baldwin lays down a case before the reader. The author witnesses everything from interracial couple persecutions to the White Caste System Disease to the homegrown terrorism of police brutality to employment discrimination to systematically enforced (and endorsed) poverty. All the tools of demonic warfare that aid in the swift corrosion and destruction of the human soul.

Incomparable beyond the shadow of any given form of doubt, James Baldwin, in his infinite penmanship, apprehends the madness of the God complex and paints a portrait of spiritual ruination exceptionally in this intensely emotional work of legendary fiction. And no genuine advocate of the urban literature class should have his or her collection minus it lest his or her collection be the poorer for it.

Five America the Ugly stars.

Cat Ellington's review of Mixed Blessings by Danielle Steel

My rating: 3 of 5 stars

Date read: March, 1996

In the wake of completing her enjoyable effort *Star*, Danielle Steel had earned new respect in me. While I wouldn't go so far as to label myself, oh, dare I say it, a "fan" of Ms. Steel's fiction, I have found a few of her scripts satisfactory enough to have appreciated my experience with reading them. Steel has a style uniquely her own: casual, laid-back, overtly contemporary. And she has garnered a myriad of serious fans who enjoy her fabled literature to a fault. Only I, personally, have yet to reach that singular affection.

Mixed Blessings, the narrative presently under review, is one of such tales. Composed in Steel's trademark contemporary vein, the dialogue had not been slow, but it also had not been what I would call "fast-paced," either.

The plot, set in California, wraps itself around three couples. They are all strangers who coincidentally marry on the same day. And although they do not know each other, they all share a common predicament. None of the newlywed wives can conceive a child because they are all barren. And because of their misfortunes, desperation troubles their fragile minds.
Here is where their legendary creator, Steel, unveils her creative vision, interweaving her cast with the same in-and-out sequence over the entire course of the plot. The author's writing shows itself approved as her ensemble

toils, even if only so effortlessly, to bring the dynamic vision to life on these pages.

Of them all, Charlie Winwood was by far my favorite, simply because I had been sympathetic towards his aim. Unfortunately, though, his wife, Beth, did not share my sentiment. My admiration for Charlie Winwood was motivated even more so by his tenacity throughout his entire trial—if one could even call it that—with a barren and hateful wife. A woman who tears down her own house with her bare hands.

HIGHLY RECOMMENDED.

Even to a discriminating thriller and action aficionado, namely myself, *Mixed Blessings* was a relatively significant read. And because there will forever dwell within me a reader who stands for the atypical romance novel, I would highly recommend Danielle Steel's *Mixed Blessings* to those fans who harbor a keen interest in the genre's contemporary counterpart – with pleasure.

Happy reading.

Cat Ellington's review of Boss: Richard J. Daley of Chicago by Mike Royko

My rating: 5 of 5 stars

Date read: April, 1996

Being a native of Chicago's South Side, *Boss: Richard J. Daley of Chicago* had been a mandatory read for me. Mike Royko, one of Chicago's Very Own, slipped on his brass knuckles and struck a fierce blow, right to the temple of my reader, with this effort. And the dialogue, hateful to the gray matter of its brain, is not one that my intellect will anytime soon forget.

Boss: Richard J. Daley of Chicago is perhaps one of the most phenomenal efforts of its respective genre, brandishing a stainless steel weapon of sharp-cutting truth and dousing the reader with a scalding hot fluid of rage-inducing Godlessness. Royko takes no prisoners, be they dead or alive, with his masterpiece. Following the precipitous climb of the infamous Richard J. Daley to his Pew of Power over Chicago, Royko sheds light on his reign as its mayor and boss of its so-called Democratic Machine.

From the setup of his everlasting witness, the beloved (at least by my standards) Royko dons his lead gloves and goes all in, jabbing with supreme uppercuts, left hooks, liver shots, and brutal head-to-body blows. Royko, a former Chicago journalist with a penchant for rocking boats—despite the identity or societal status of any given vessel's skipper—goes straight for the symbolic carotid artery of one of the most powerful political figures in American history.

Indeed, Mike Royko's *Boss: Richard J. Daley of Chicago* is not a narrative fit for the one who offends without difficulty.

Where the spirit of this testimony is concerned, many readers will regard it well: for the inhumane exposé is at once a vicious, devastating, hard-hearted, bitter, racist, anti-Semitic, horrifying, malicious, evil, and ungodly work of nonfiction. And it will forever be perceived as such among those of its endearing genus.

Five non-sugar-coated stars.

Cat Ellington's review of Boots of the Oppressor by LaMorris Richmond

My rating: 5 of 5 stars

Date read: May, 1996

I read the first issue of *Boots of the Oppressor* in April of 1993. And I am compelled to admit that the graphic novel is a release most maniacal and merciless.

LaMorris Richmond's *Boots of the Oppressor* is a landmark in its class, a distinction in its own right, and not merely a graphic narrative prepared to suffer the one who is easily offended gladly.
The novel highlights the horror of racism in America and the faulty foundation on which it stands. Richmond exposes the demonic wrath of home-grown terrorism, tyranny, and the cruel dictator-like afflictions suffered by tens of millions of African slaves—and their future generations—at the hands of the European Settlement in America.

Though emotionally dislodging, *Boots of the Oppressor* is an educational must-read, no matter your culture.
A tightly wrapped and sadistic sucker punch of truth, LaMorris Richmond's *Boots of the Oppressor* is a graphic worthy of tour de force ranking.

Five true-to-its-legend stars.

**Cat Ellington's review of Along Came a Spider by
James Patterson**

My rating: 5 of 5 stars

Date read: April, 1996

Along Came a Spider was my introduction to the
outstanding literature of Mr. James Patterson. It had been
my husband who'd handed me my very first Patterson
effort, being it *Along Came a Spider*. And inspired by my
hubby's rave review of the work, I commenced to read it.
Brilliant in its plot, loaded with action and suspense, and
well-rounded in character development, *Along Came a
Spider*, the inceptive release in the ever-popular Alex
Cross series, is a magnum opus of veritable ingenuity.

Chaos seeps out of its miserable cocoon after Washington,
DC homicide investigator Alex Cross, currently
investigating the deaths of three African-American people,
gets lured into a game of cat-and-mouse with a murderer,
kidnapper, and sociopath named Gary Murphy. Murphy is
a likely suspect in the killings, and Cross needs to hunt him
down. Murphy is also the suspect in the kidnappings of two
rich White children, among other yet unsolved murders in
the DC area.
Before long, Alex Cross has to put his first investigation on
hold. The chain-of-command wants the kidnappings
investigated first - a command that does not go over well
with Alex Cross. And as the bodies pile up, a game of
cat-and-mouse gets underway. And Alex Cross will be
pushed to the limit. But who will reign as the victor –

especially when one's opponents are jealousy, envy, and rage?

Along Came a Spider is flawless. It is a mesmerizing thriller that will keep the reader engrossed until the turning of the final page, and it is above and beyond worthy of my loftiest recommendation.
Along Came a Spider is a must-read, indeed.

Five dying-to-be-famous stars.

Cat Ellington's review of Red Dragon by Thomas Harris

My rating: 5 of 5 stars

Date read: August, 1996

Do you believe in the Tooth Fairy?

The blood-curdling inspiration behind 1992's "The Silence of the Lambs," *Red Dragon*, dexterously composed by the proficient Thomas Harris, is the hard-to-put-down originator of one Dr. Hannibal Lecter.

For those of you, my fellow readers, who are familiar with the notable artwork, I honestly don't believe that any of you will ever gaze upon the William Blake masterpiece, "The Great Red Dragon," ca. 1805, in the same way again after you've concluded this fiction. At least you won't if, like me, you share an undying passion for art.

Red Dragon is a skillfully-penned and electrifying horror that will invoke in its reader paralyzing fear and anxiety. And while I do indeed recommend the effort to those enthusiasts of the separate horror and thriller genres, I would only advise that you consume the account during the daytime hours – as the same is not prose intended for the easily dismayed.

Five utility-pole-repairing stars.

Chapter 2
Through the Valleys of Nurturing

Cat Ellington's review of Night Shift by Stephen King

My rating: 5 of 5 stars

Date read: October, 1996

The first time that I read Stephen King's *Night Shift* was during the summer of 1994. And the second time I read Stephen King's *Night Shift* was in October of 1996. There is just something special about the literature of the fabled Stephen King. His work has always gotten me right here. I find pleasurable comfort in his writing - if that makes any sense. I have always felt a sort of affinity with his one-of-a-kind narratives. Many of them have brought me extreme joy. And *Night Shift*, that solitary compilation featuring a considerable collection of some of King's most spectacular short stories, is no exception.

As a collective body, *Night Shift* is a bone-chilling, heart-in-your-mouth page-turner brought to the reader by the beloved Master of Horror himself, and includes such short stories as *The Mangler* (one of my all-time favorites), *Sometimes They Come Back* (utterly creepy), *Gray Matter*, *Children of the Corn*, and *The Boogeyman*, among a fine class of others.

Although I have stamped each short story in the collection with an individual rating, I have rendered the overall effort with a 5-star rating based on my separate list of pros and cons.

__The Works with My Ratings__

Jerusalem's Lot: 5 out of 5 stars

Graveyard Shift: 5 out of 5 stars

Night Surf: 3 out of 5 stars

I Am the Doorway: 5 out of 5 stars

The Mangler: 5 out of 5 stars

The Boogeyman: 5 out of 5 stars

Gray Matter: 5 out of 5 stars

Battleground: 4 out of 5 stars

Trucks: 5 out of 5 stars

Sometimes They Come Back: 5 out of 5 stars

Strawberry Spring: 3 out of 5 stars

The Ledge: 5 out of 5 stars

The Lawnmower Man: 5 out of 5 stars

Quitters, Inc.: 5 out of 5 stars

I Know What You Need: 3 out of 5 stars

Children of the Corn: 5 out of 5 stars

The Last Run on the Ladder: 2 out of 5 stars

The Man Who Loved Flowers: 5 out of 5 stars

One for the Road: 3 out of 5 stars

The Woman in the Room: 3 out of 5 stars

I had no problem reading *Night Shift* for a second time, as the account comprises several novellas that hardly bore. Stephen King is undoubtedly magnificent. And his *Night Shift*, an opus in its respect, is a definite must-read for the true horror fan.

Five scared to death stars.

Cat Ellington's review of the Highwaymen by Ken Auletta

My rating: 5 of 5 stars

Date read: March, 1997

K-Man and the "Masters of the Universe."

Ken Auletta, a celebrated journalist with a first-rate history in the New York media, gathers the powers that be in the communications industry for a one-on-one of tea-spilling, position-jockeying, verbal-feuding, backstabbing, money-worshipping, and an all-out covetous battle to be that ultimate titan, even the head tariff hoarder on the information superhighway. Hence, the title of his must-read exposé, *The Highwaymen: Warriors of the Information Superhighway.*

Incorporated from several Auletta's *New Yorker* articles during the 1990s, *The Highwaymen: Warriors of the Information Superhighway* features an illustrious cast of nonfictional players who dwell at the helms of television networks, cable networks, computer networks, telephone publishing houses, Hollywood studios, etc. Said entities include Viacom, Time Warner, News Corporation, Microsoft, Disney, Telecommunications, Incorporated, etc.

But wait. There's more.

The juiciest and most tender meat of this splendid work, penned by the clever Auletta, had been his Barbara Walters-like interviews with the head honchos themselves. Yes, finally coming out from behind the curtains are none other than Michael Eisner, Bill Gates, Ted Turner, Gerald Levin, Rupert Murdoch, Sumner Redstone, Edgar Bronfman, Jr., Michael Ovitz, Barry Diller, John Malone, etc.

The Highwaymen: Warriors of the Information Superhighway was indeed one of the most informative and devoutly interesting narratives of nonfiction that I have ever had the gratification of reading. And that is not at all surprising considering who its journalistic father is.

Five power-hungry stars.

Cat Ellington's review of Accident by Danielle Steel

My rating: 5 of 5 stars

Date read: May, 1997

WHEN FATE CHALLENGES FAITH.

Danielle Steel is legendary in contemporary fiction. And while I am not so much of an ardent Steel enthusiast, I have had the opportunity to read a few of her efforts that were relatively satisfying to my reader, including *Accident*, the anecdote presently under review.

With a solid plot, setting, and carefully selected cast, the script comes alive, introducing the reader to both its leading lady Page Clarke and her extremely dislikable husband, Brad. The couple lives a reasonably comfortable life with their two children Andrew, 7, and Allyson, 15, near San Francisco. The Clarke clan does alright by societal standards. And the wealthy lot are taking a cakewalk along the path of life when, on one fateful night while out joyriding with her best friend and two teenage boys, Allyson suffers extensive injuries as the result of a head-on collision with another vehicle on the expressway. The popular teen sustains irreparable damage to her once remarkably-beautiful, young face. And from there, their lives spiral out of control.
Out of nowhere, tragedy strikes the Clarke household like a fiery serpent, tearing apart cashmere and silk, fine wool, and handcrafted embroidery. And the previously proud and privileged Clarke family unit will have their faith put to the test in the most vicious of ways.

A MOTHER'S LOVE.

A very emotional read, *Accident* is graced with fascinating dialogue heavily dependent upon faith, strength, and hope. These are their challenges. And the frustration runs deep.

Page Clarke is a trooper and a woman who loves her children with the whole heart, even unconditionally. And playing witness to her many trials, my reader couldn't help but admire her strength and her courage through them all. I loved this character. And so will you.

With *Accident*, Danielle Steel not only commanded but double-dared me. And it is her penmanship here that is meritable of my highest recommendation.

Five nothing like a mother's love stars.

Cat Ellington's review of Misery by Stephen King

My rating: 5 of 5 stars

Date read: July, 1997

"I'm your number one fan."
—Annie Wilkes

The most dreaded compliment paid to any real life novelist, especially in the aftermath of Stephen King's *Misery*.

A psychological horror, *Misery*, the title of the book, takes its namesake from Misery Chastain, the heroine of author Paul Sheldon's romance novels. But on the pages of Stephen King's eerie-spirited narrative, the plot unfurls in a wintry Colorado setting where the famous author, Sheldon, is holed up and enjoying his fancy accommodations at a five-star hotel. Sheldon has checked himself into the swanky lodge to obtain a little bit of quiet peace while he puts the final touches on the highly-anticipated manuscript for his latest book. And as the scenes roll, Paul Sheldon, the famous author extraordinaire, obtains his desired peace. Sheldon is enjoying his fame and fortune to the fullest extent.

All is well until the self-confident author ventures out into the treacherous elements. A terrible accident on the snowy roads befalls the great Paul Sheldon, leaving him stranded and both of his legs injured where he is unable to move. But rather than an ambulance—equipped with a paramedic unit—arriving on the scene to aid and assist the wounded writer, Paul is found by another individual with a highly trained degree in the medical profession: a former nurse named Annie.

Misery is bitter cold in both climate and spirit. And it ranks at a statuesque level on the totem pole of King's finest (and most frightening) masterworks. For a surety, Misery is bold enough to stand the trying test of time. And no true pundit of horror should have his or her collection void of it.

Five dirty birdy stars.

Cat Ellington's review of The World's Best-Kept Beauty Secrets: What Really Works in Beauty, Diet & Fashion by Diane Irons

My rating: 5 of 5 stars

Date Read: August, 1997

Diane Irons' *The World's Best-Kept Beauty Secrets* is one astounding health, beauty, and styling reference guide! Initially published in 1997, the first edition is a precise must-have for the beauty passionate in every woman.

It had been during the summer of 1997—two weeks following its release, to be exact—that I borrowed this highly knowledgeable self-help reference from a Chicago Public Library branch to obtain a better feel for its contents. And immediately upon returning the guide to the same library a few days later, I decided that I needed to purchase my very own copy. And I did. The large, glossy paperback deserved to have a place amongst my many other reference guides, and it was well-received.

The World's Best-Kept Beauty Secrets had been one of my beauty buff's most exciting purchases during that time. And I will love it forever. No sooner had I completed the effort than I commenced to compose a review of it – in honor of its proficiency and admirable detail. Irons did her homework, even a ton of research for this edition. And I appreciate her the more so for it.

To every woman keen on the art of natural beauty and the rewarding benefits of natural skincare, *The World's*

Best-Kept Beauty Secrets comes exceedingly recommended. Here's to a naturally gorgeous you!

Five freely shared stars.

Chapter 3
Over the Hills of Encouragement

Cat Ellington's review of The Face of Fear by Dean Koontz

My rating: 5 of 5 stars

Date read: October, 1997

To this very day, even its description still gives me chills. A brilliant tale of crippling terror is *The Face of Fear*. Initially published in 1977, Koontz penned the work under the pseudonym Brian Coffey and drove home a classic masterwork of utter trepidation.

Imagine, if you will, being trapped inside of a dark New York skyscraper, on its top floor with absolutely no way out amid a blizzard, all while being hunted down like prey by a ruthless and murderous psychopath armed with extra-sharp cutlery.
That is the horrifying predicament in which our leading man, Graham Harris, and his girlfriend, Connie, find themselves, as the shivering pages of this blatantly disturbing psychological horror roll themselves over.

The homicidal butcher is mutilating young women. And Graham Harris knows this because Graham Harris is blessed—or cursed, depending upon how one perceives it—with a rather strange ability that affords him a firsthand witness to grisly murders as they're happening. Not only can the clairvoyant Graham observe heinous murders in progress, but he's also able to envision them before they occur.

Now the killer is on the elevator in Graham's building. And he's on his way up to Graham's floor. Graham can sense the monster coming, but he and Connie have no way out. The blizzard outside screams and shrieks through the soot-black darkness. And the two of them are about to come face-to-face with the longest and most terrifying night of their lives.

The Face of Fear is a heart-pounding and petrifying game of hide-and-seek that will have the reader turning the pages way into the wee hours. And it is not a dialogue that I am inclined to neglect to recommend. But whatever you do, please, do not look down.

Five heart palpitation-producing stars.

Cat Ellington's review of Work in Progress by Tony Schwartz and Michael Eisner

My rating: 4 of 5 stars

Date read: September, 1999

Work in Progress is an autobiographical witness from the man to whom many had referred as 'villainous' throughout his twenty-one-year reign as top boss at the Walt Disney Company: Michael Eisner. There were even a few folks who joked that the "D" in Eisner's middle name stood for "Disney," when in fact, it stands for "Dammann," the maiden name of Eisner's mother, respectively.

Those petty, albeit hilarious, jabs aside, Michael Eisner, the leading man in the nonfiction currently under examination, presents his life story to the reader who has eyes to see in this relatively fascinating account, co-authored with Tony Schwartz (*Trump: The Art of the Deal*). And I must admit that I initially found the title inappropriate considering that Eisner, a decades-long influencer in the entertainment and business worlds alike, couldn't possibly have a damn thing more to prove. But apparently, he does.

Surprisingly, there were more than a few shared trivia facts about Mr. Eisner that we, the people outside of his inner circle, never knew about him until now.
For starters, Eisner's great-grandfather, Sigmund Eisner, was a renowned manufacturer who founded the Sigmund Eisner Company, the exclusive maker of the uniforms for the Boy Scouts of America. Eisner's maternal grandfather, Milton Dammann, after a career of shining shoes on the streets of Washington, DC, worked his way through college

before enrolling at Georgetown Law. And in all due time, Milton Eisner would climb the corporate ladder to become President of The American Safety Razor Company.

A very prominent secular Jewish clan indeed, the Eisners. And where his culture comes into focus, the Park Avenue-raised business mogul is challenged to recall many happy memories. Emotional about his Jewish upbringing, Eisner confesses to Schwartz about being tempted to hate himself for being Jewish due to the constant anti-Semitic bullying that he had unfortunately been subjected to all too often during his era of youth. And as the pages of his autobiographical witness continue to unfurl—revealing more details—so does the man named Michael Eisner come to life from behind the closed-in walls of the so-called "Happiest Place on Earth."

Overall, *Work in Progress* is a fine effort by Tony Schwartz and his subject, Michael Eisner. And I truly enjoyed it - but only to a point. Because the witness lacked depth at times, not to mention many "questionable" professions, I am inclined to settle it with a four-star rating.

Happy reading, all.

Cat Ellington's review of Cows on Parade by Mary Ellen Sullivan

My rating: 5 of 5 stars

Date read: October, 1999

If there is one city world-renowned for its inimitable passion for the Arts—including its astonishing displays of ridiculously brilliant street art—that city is Chicago. The gorgeous Second City is forever outdoing herself, with each new public art exhibit going out of its way to being just a whole lot better than the one preceding it. Case in point: Cows on Parade (1999).

Only after its remarkable debut in Chicago, during the summer of 1999, did the captivating public art exhibit become a worldwide phenomenon. And it was beloved during its tenure. Set in various locations around the city, the decorated cows each had a theme that honored many Chicago legends. Like the Marshall Fields cow, for example, which donned a bow-tied stack of the department store's gift boxes atop its back: the design also featured those famous words of its founding father: Give the lady what she wants. That particular cow had been my absolute favorite one of them all: for she was simply a beauty in the eye of my beholder.

Cows on Parade had been a stroke of genius. And many Chicagoans, myself included, cried like newborn babies when the matchless public art exhibit completed its run in our adored city: for we were loath to see them go.

Co-authored with Simon Koenig and Herbert Berchtold, respectively, Mary Ellen Sullivan's *Cows on Parade in Chicago* is a phenomenal keepsake. And it will continue to amaze its readers (both old and new) each time they find themselves engrossed in the effort's glossy pages, not to mention the captivating history of its subject matter. A must-have, indeed!

For the native Chicagoan, as well as for those tourists who had been fortunate enough to view the display during its four-month run, Mary Ellen Sullivan's *Cows on Parade in Chicago* is the perfect cure for nostalgia.

Five grazing stars.

Cat Ellington's review of Chicago (Lonely Planet Guide) by Ryan Ver Berkmoes

My rating: 5 of 5 stars

Date read: February, 2000

An exciting read for the aboriginal Chicagoan and an immensely resourceful reference guide for the tourist, Ryan "We miss ya in da Chi, Ry!" Ver Berkmoes strikes solid gold with this stunning and glossy paperback. *Chicago (Lonely Planet Guide)* covers nearly every corner of the unparalleled Windy City. Only after Ver Berkmoes, a storied journalist, parted ways with Chicago to live abroad in Europe did those of us Chicagoans who were familiar with his finely-written guides create the moniker in his honor. It had been our way of showing one of our very own how much love we fostered for him and our vast appreciation for his various contributions in journalism.

Ver Berkmoes' coveted effort, *Chicago (Lonely Planet Guide)*, is a commanding legend in its respect because, as the old saying goes, "Chicago is world-famous for its architecture." And Ryan Ver Berkmoes generously covers the city's dynamic skyline on the pages of this magnificent reference. Also, one cannot reside in or even visit Chicago and expect there to be an outlet for boredom, as the place is just too huge and too lively.

Be ye a native, or be ye a non-native, so long as this information-packed guide is in your possession, I reckon that you will never need another. For it includes just about everything one's heart can desire for enjoying time spent in Chicago: architecture, dining, museums, sightseeing tours, blues clubs, jazz clubs, nightlife, sporting events, and so much more.

Ryan Ver Berkmoes' enthralling *Chicago (Lonely Planet Guide)* also incorporates a *Facts for the Visitor* section (which in itself spans 30 pages), a *Things To Do and See* section, as well as a *Places to Stay* section. And each segment is more than delighted to cater to the city's ever-constant tourists.

Now, lest we forget that Chicago is a city of neighborhoods—77, to be exact—Ryan guides the reader through each unique community - all bordered by the South, North, and West sides. And, of course, after such a lengthy tour, you may find yourself working up a hearty appetite. But don't worry, Ryan's got you covered.

What is your edible pleasure? Deep-dish pizza? Pit-smoked barbecue ribs? Gyros? Pierogies? Vegetarian fare? Soul Food? Perfectly cooked corned beef and cabbage? Greek salads? Italian Beef? Vienna Beef Franks? Or maybe even some mozzarella sticks with a side of marinara sauce? Garrett's popcorn? How about a platter of fried chicken from Harold's Chicken Shack? Or some take-out from Grand Chinese Kitchen? Whatever your taste buds may crave, Chicago will be able to oblige. She'll even make you welcome to a hefty slice of her famous Eli's cheesecake (smothered in cherries or strawberries) for dessert. Oh, I do declare.

When in the city of Chicago, you reserve the right to splurge. And no one, especially not any of its many tourists, should have his or her reference-guide collection minus this precious gem, penned by the well-traveled and dearly beloved Ryan Ver Berkmoes. Indeed, *Chicago*

(Lonely Planet Guide) is a loftily recommended must-have for you all.

Five make yourselves at home stars.

Cat Ellington's review of Rum Punch by Elmore Leonard

My rating: 5 of 5 stars

Date read: April, 2000

If there is a better word than "*outstanding*," let it apply here. Where the great Elmore Leonard writes, trust that there will be a great deal of delight, even a mightily blessed script decorated with a phenomenally talented cast of players for the dear reader's psyche to ingest. Like the celebrated author's masterwork, *Rum Punch*, for instance.

The inspiration behind Quentin Tarantino's cult classic film, *Jackie Brown*, *Rum Punch* stars a forty-four-year-old airline stewardess named Jackie Burke. Burke, recruited by a murderous gunrunner named Ordell Robbie to smuggle his illegal monies into the United States from Jamaica, does so via her scheduled flights. And the setup, in operation for an extended time, is winging it along a butter-smooth trajectory, or so it seems until the feds arrive at the airport just as Jackie Burke is returning to the States from the Island with Ordell's blood money buried neatly in her carry-on bag.

The worst is that the ATF apprehends Jackie and then interrogates the stewardess further, threatening to destroy her by way of job loss and prison time - unless she sacrifices herself to assist them in their scheme to capture the menacing and blood-congealing Ordell. But with time, Ordell Robbie would learn about the arrest. And fearing that she will give in and hand him over to the ATF agents on a polished silver platter, Ordell immediately slithers into self-preservation mode. For him, the plan is to either kill or go to prison. And in his case, that would be for life. And Ordell Robbie does not intend to spend what's left of his worthless life behind anyone's prison bars; therefore, he must first use, and then end, the stewardess. Of course, Jackie Burke is fully aware that her life is in danger at the hands of the cold-blooded Ordell. And for that reason, she concocts a scheme of her own. She will hoodwink Ordell and the Feds and get away with all the cash. Or she will get shot, twice, in the back of her head—by Ordell—trying.

Louis Gara and Max Cherry co-star in this gripping oeuvre of thrilling, nail-biting, and on-the-edge-of-your-seat suspense, delivered to the reader most spectacularly, courtesy of the irrefutably incomparable Elmore Leonard.

Rum Punch is a knock-out punch of literary ingenuity. A legend in the highly-regarded crime thriller genre, the novel is more than worthy of my recommendation, particularly to those many diehard upholders of its respective class.

Five big man ting stars.

Cat Ellington's review of The Brethren by John Grisham

My rating: 3 of 5 stars

Date read: June, 2000

He ain't heavy, he's my brother.

Three former judges, all incarcerated in a federal Penitentiary for crimes committed in violation of their Oaths of Office, star in *The Brethren*, one of John Grisham's more sluggish efforts. The lawless trio holds "mock trials" behind the claustrophobic walls of Trumble, a maximum-security prison in the state of Florida. They also have established a stratagem in which they operate as a unit to blackmail monetary spoils from rich, gay men—particularly those distinguished and prominent political figures in Washington, DC—by threatening to expose the secrets of their alternative lifestyles.

After intimidating their victims into paying them large sums of money to keep their sordid secrets safe, the three judges go one step further. They send Trevor Carson, their attorney, to deposit the dirty money in an offshore account. Of course, they pay him a small fee for his sleazy services. And the beat goes on. But is there truly a pot of gold at the end of every proverbial rainbow? The Brethren soon find out when their grift swaggers its pride across the merciless threshold of one Teddy Maynard.

Though not one of the great Grisham's more superior narratives, *The Brethren* still has teeth sharp enough to leave an imprint on the reader's psyche. And the only flaw in this storyline? Its pace. It simply traveled along the literary path a bit too slowly – lacking momentum and inducing frustrated fatigue in my reader. But despite that small con, I would still recommend *The Brethren* to those innumerable pundits of the cherished legal thriller genre. Yes, but of course, I would.

Happy reading, everyone.

Chapter 4
Along the Paths of Love and Support

Cat Ellington's review of The House of Gucci: A Sensational Story of Murder, Madness, Glamour, and Greed by Sara Gay Forden

My rating: 5 of 5 stars

Date read: September, 2000

Sara Gay Forden displays—before the reader—one helluva scandalous exposé in *The House of Gucci: A Sensational Story of Murder, Madness, Glamour, and Greed*. On these exclusive pages, the author whisks her viewers away, on a whirlwind excursion, to the luxuriously exotic Florence, Italy. There, she reveals a page-turning witness of the mayhem that ravaged one of the greatest—and most undeniably opulent—family dynasties that ever established upon the well-attired rock of the fashion industry: the Gucci family.

This remarkable tell-all ventures behind the scenes of the high-fashion world to divulge the fascinating accounts surrounding the murder of the extra extravagant heir to the Gucci empire—Maurizio Gucci—allegedly at the bejeweled hands of a woman spurned. The same being his estranged ex-wife, Patrizia Reggiani.

The question was asked: 'Did she kill him? Or didn't she?'

Find out the answer in this nail-biting invitation to sit as a symbolic spectator in the Italian courtroom as the so-called "Second Trial of the Century" unfolds itself before your very eyes.

Dear reader, if you fancy mystery, suspense, drama, thrills, avarice, deceit, intrigue, lavish jet-set living, sex and seduction, Horsebit detail, Interlocking G Ornaments, green and red Signature Webs, Italian leather loafers, classic handbags, and stylish ready-to-wear, then you will not want to be without *The House of Gucci: A Sensational Story of Murder, Madness, Glamour, and Greed*. For said disclosure is Sara Gay Forden's ultimate magnum opus.

Five Envy Me stars.

**Cat Ellington's review of How Stella Got Her Groove
Back by Terry McMillan**

My rating: 3 of 5 stars

Date read: February, 2001

Ms. Terry McMillan, one dearly beloved and respected, is
meritable of the highest grade that there is to render for her
much-read and legendary literature. And while I would be
among the first to rate the narrative presently under review
at the top of the scale with five stars, unfortunately, I
cannot. Because *How Stella Got Her Groove Back* didn't
ensnare my reader in quite the same way that *Waiting to
Exhale* did.

McMillan gives it all she has here with a solid storyline, a
stunning setting, and a better than ever cast. And *How
Stella Got Her Groove Back* would've been a terrifically
perfect romance had it not been so slow-paced. That said,
I would undoubtedly recommend the fiction to a myriad of
urban romance enthusiasts, but I will stop short of issuing it
five stars.

Happy reading, all.

Cat Ellington's review of The Grifters by Jim Thompson

My rating: 5 of 5 stars

Date read: May, 2001

The Grifters equals Gritty, ravenous, icy, ferocious, turbulent, exceptional, and ruthless storytelling.

One of the greatest novels in the genre of noir fiction, Jim Thompson's masterwork is the same tale that served as the inspiration behind the Stephen Frears-directed cinematic oeuvre of the same name. Listed among an elite class of my favorite novels in literary history, *The Grifters* was indeed Thompson's sledgehammer to the reader's psyche.
The tale, smothered in a gravy of bloodlust, greed, deception, corruption, incest, and murder, is a five-star jewel in its respective set: for its capacity can stand the test of time.

Be there any femme fatale in fiction like the one named Lilly Dillon? Indeed, they are few and far between. For Lilly is a femme fatale for the literary record books. She is a dame who has cherry red ice water flowing through her veins. Lilly Dillon is as brutal as they come, and for a certainty, she is not a character fit for the faint: for I have yet to encounter one who has read *The Grifters* and is inclined to disagree with my praise of it. And I would recommend reading it to anyone who loves hard-boiled noir.

Brought to you by the great Master of Noir Fiction, even incomparable Jim Thompson, *The Grifters* is a legend to behold.

Five across the board stars.

Cat Ellington's review of She's Come Undone by Wally Lamb

My rating: 5 of 5 stars

Date read: July, 2001

While reading Wally Lamb's *She's Come Undone*—a better than fantastic effort, I might add—there were two things about which I could not cease thinking: one, The Guess Who's classic rock recording of the same title, and, two, the Lee Phillips-directed film, "The Girl Most Likely To," ca. 1973.

A highly relatable story, *She's Come Undone* is a coming-of-age tale about a girl named Dolores Price who battles childhood obesity and a ton of mental anguish. Everyone seems to be cruel to Dolores, even her wayward mother. And with few friends and no emotional support, Dolores comes undone.

She undertakes a great deal of physical and emotional pain in her hard-won life. And I, for one, loved her tenacity and her courage to carry on. She believes in herself, despite the hate she receives. And she is a superstar as far as I am concerned. It was towards Dolores that I felt overcome with such a considerable amount of empathy. Why? Well, because I also battled the bulge as a child. I felt Dolores, and I understood her pain. Dolores Price is a heroine for every chubby girl. And I will love her forever, even if only in her fictive existence.

She's Come Undone is a work of fiction that I strongly recommend, whether the reader has ever struggled with obesity or even if they know someone else who has. Honestly, it is no surprise that Oprah Winfrey selected this singular narrative, declaring it a must-read to her world-famous book club. Wally Lamb should be incredibly proud.

Five coming-out-of-her-shell stars.

Cat Ellington's review of The Killer Inside Me by Jim Thompson

My rating: 5 of 5 stars

Date read: October, 2001

Jim Thompson's *The Killer Inside Me* is an extraordinarily penned account of American Noir fiction. And it provides a sufficient amount of proof as to why I love the literature of its eminent authorship on the statuesque level that I do.

Hard-boiled in every definition of the term, *The Killer Inside Me* is bone-chilling cold, both spiritually and humanly. Meet Lou Ford. For those of you new to the work, that's deputy Lou Ford of small-town Texas. As the dark pages of this noir proceed themselves, deputy Lou takes the proverbial witness stand to testify in his defense. And though deputy Lou Ford "appears" clean-cut on the surface, what lies beneath his physical façade, in the depths of his embittered soul, is a treacherous predator prone to perversity, pedophilia, depravity, and murderous rage. Deputy Lou Ford. He is the petrifying epitome of a practicing sociopath.

On the deceptive contrary, deputy Lou is a dearly loved fixture in his embraced community. Deputy Lou is well-known and enviably respected by both the unlawful and law-abiding alike: fellow law enforcement officers, entrepreneurs, big-time criminals, small-time criminals, wannabe criminals, close-knit families, academic staff members, etc. Everybody loves deputy Lou.
Oh, how dangerous it is to be flesh-minded!

A timeless cult classic is the awe-inspiring Jim Thompson's *The Killer Inside Me*. And if ye shall be a reader who has acquired a literary taste for the masterful American Noir genre, not owning a copy of said narrative would only represent a negligent disservice to your cherished library.

Five killer charm stars.

Chapter 5
Across the Plains of Commitment

Cat Ellington's review of Freaky Deaky by Elmore Leonard

My rating: 5 of 5 stars

Date read: January, 2002

If the groovy title of this outta sight classic doesn't purvey to the reader even the slightest hint of what the storyline therein is all about, then I couldn't possibly imagine what would. But know that when you go Elmore Leonard, you can expect to be his private passenger on one helluva hallucinatory and entertaining thrill ride. As one would probably suspect, the description also pertains to the great man's precious literary jewel, *Freaky Deaky*.

In this psychedelic and outrageously hilarious Leonard effort, the plot trips itself out around a motley crew of 1960s rebels who gather together on behalf of one common cause: forming a bomb-making enterprise for profit. And out to put an end to their madness is one of Detroit City's finest lawmen, sergeant Chris Mankowski. But to bring this group of homegrown terrorists to nothing, the no-nonsense sergeant Mankowski must first infiltrate their maniacal organization. And no sooner than he does do things get bloody and murderous and callous and disgustingly scandalous.

Elmore Leonard's *Freaky Deaky* boasts not only great dialogue but also a repulsive cast of loathsome characters who add a generous helping of pizzazz to the Leonard script with their mind-bending performances. These would include an alcoholic automobile heir, a former Black Panther Party member, a grifter pretending to be a nursemaid, an ex-con bomber, and a bomb expert. A bunch of heathens, indeed. The best thing going for them is the gorgeous Greta, otherwise known as Ginger - a true-blue spirit with whom Chris Mankowski falls madly in love.

Set in a blustery Detroit, *Freaky Deaky* is by far one of the most interest-gripping plots to bear the authorship of the superlative Elmore Leonard. And it is to the entire fandom of the mystery-thriller genre that I would approvingly recommend it.

Five PCP-affected stars.

Cat Ellington's review of Lucky You by Carl Hiaasen

My rating: 5 of 5 stars

Date read: March, 2002

What would you do if you won a $28 million Lotto jackpot?

In this gut-busting Carl Hiaasen masterpiece, that is the amount of money a Lotto ticket purchased by Ms. JoLayne Lucks, an African-American veterinarian assistant living in the Sunshine State, is worth.

The leading lady of this exceptional crime caper, turtle enthusiast JoLayne Lucks goes into a convenience store to buy a game ticket. She plays the same Lotto numbers that she has consistently played over a very lengthy course of time, and then bam! Just like that, the undeniably lovable JoLayne Lucks finally hits it big. However, there is only one small problem. Another winning ticket matching the same numbers is out there. And the owners of that ticket are none other than the terrible twosome of Bodean "Bode" Gazzer and his close-as-skin best friend, Chub, a self-loathing duo of unemployed White supremacists, hell-bent on chaos. And boy, do they encounter it. As are the rules of any state Lottery system, the $28 million purse won by the stars of *Lucky You* has to be split evenly down the middle. A nice directive considering that $14 million would be a challenge to earn in a single lifetime. But even still, the two confederate flag-waving never-do-wells, Bode and Chub, want the entire pot for themselves. And when they both learn that the other winning ticket holder is an African-American woman, all sides-splittin' hell breaks loose.

Laughing out loud is not good enough an expression to describe the reaction that Carl Hiaasen's *Lucky You* is guaranteed to bring forth from within the reader, as the same is an unputdownable phenomenon in its respective genre of the crime caper. Hiaasen's authorship is nothing short of genius. And it is for this very reason that he has earned an everlasting place on the exclusive list of my all-time favorite novelists: extraordinary vision and penmanship.

Five big winner stars.

Cat Ellington's review of The Partner by John Grisham

My rating: 2 of 5 stars

Date read: July, 2002

In brief, I strove to make myself enjoy this book due to its authorship. But no matter how much I tried to force myself to like this book, regardless of its authorship, the feeling of admiration only forced itself to elude me concerning it.

As much as I love and respect the literary fiction of John Grisham, the undisputed Master of the Legal Thriller, *The Partner* was an extreme disappointment to my reader. Does the effort possess any potential? Perhaps some readers may think so. But to the action-packed thriller lover in my reader, the pace of *The Partner* only indicated creative fatigue upon the otherwise dexterous hand of its legendary father; therefore, the spirit of the anecdote could only manage to bring about fatigue within me, its reader.

Would I still recommend *The Partner* to those readers who love legal thrillers, regardless of my lackluster experience with it? I most certainly would, as to each his own.

Happy reading, all.

Cat Ellington's review of Chicago Then & Now by Elizabeth McNulty

My rating: 5 of 5 stars

Date read: September, 2002

Chicago's past gives way to the present in this, Elizabeth McNulty's glorious pictorial, *Chicago Then & Now*. The large hardcover edition proudly shows a fine collection of glossy before-and-after photos of the beautiful city. And it also features an in-depth dialogue of historical facts that pertain to its world-renowned architecture.

The structures featured on these fascinating pages include the Rookery, the Art Institute, the Museum of Science and Industry, Wacker Drive, Wabash Avenue, State Street, the Clarke and Glessner houses (on the South Side), the Magnificent Mile, the Field Museum, Wrigley Field, U.S. Cellular Field (Comiskey Park), the CTA Rapid Transit system, the Water Tower, and so on.

Any Chicago landmark building that is indeed a Chicago landmark building makes a vivid appearance on these must-read pages. And this reference is a must-have! Ridiculously photogenic is the city of Chicago, among those most preeminent in the world. And a hearty helping of kudos is to be rendered to Ms. Elizabeth McNulty for a fascinating job well done.

Chicago Then and Now is not a pictorial reference guide that any singular devotee of pictorials should have his or her collection absent of, as it is an admirable study, not only for Chicago's native child but also her out-of-towner.

Five sturdily built stars.

Cat Ellington's review of Basket Case by Carl Hiaasen

My rating: 5 of 5 stars

Date read: December, 2002

"If you don't own your masters, your masters will own
you."
—Prince Rogers Nelson

Despite a sluggish start, which is uncharacteristic of its
ingenious father, *Basket Case* is a crime caper/murder
mystery for the record books – or at least it becomes so
after the dialogue has eaten its Wheaties. An inducer of
gut-exploding humor, Carl Hiaasen's *Basket Case* is a
twisted little yarn about the crooked-as-a-barrel-of-snakes
music industry. And what could be more fitting for such a
topic than a wild man rock star?

The boisterously loud and proud plot orbits around the
death of a world-famous recording artist named Jimmy
Stoma. And before his untimely death, Stoma had been the
front man of a heavy metal outfit appropriately named the
Slut Puppies. Stoma was also the husband of Cleo Rio, a
kitty-flasher and equally famous personality in popular
music. The world-prominent pop music superstar, Cleo
Rio, is now a grieving widow in public mourning following
the mysterious death of her wild man hubby, Stoma – or so
she seems to be.
Enter our leading man Jack Tagger. Jack is an obit writer
for the fictive Florida Union-Register. And with time, he will
interview the grieving widow of Jimmy Stoma. The same
grieving widow who initially reported that her husband's
death resulted from a scuba-diving expedition gone awry

while the couple was vacationing in the Bahamas. Rio's account of the events that lead up to Jimmy's early death sounds legitimate enough by Tagger's estimate. But Jimmy Stoma's surviving sister, Janet, is not buying Cleo's witness, no matter how reasonably priced. Soon, Janet's plaguing doubts about Cleo Rio begin to take effect on Jack Tagger. And rather than staying in his quiet lane as an obit writer for a newspaper owned and operated by a man he hates with a scornful passion, Jack Tagger decides to do something else more exciting, more self-fulfilling. He takes it upon himself to embark on a vigilante-style investigation into the shocking death of one of the world's most recognized and endeared so-called rock gods. But what the everyday commoner, Jack Tagger, fails to understand is that he is about to dive, headfirst, into the deep, croc-infested swamp of the music industry. And for his person of general public status, it will not be well upon impact.

As the notorious plot proceeds to unfold and make an entrance into its own, one of the most hilarious and sadistic efforts about the record business to date shows itself awesomely approved. So despite a slow start, *Basket Case* eventually finds its footing, carrying the reader on its back through a wild-and-crazy haze of uproariously entertaining fun, even to the very end. And if you know the wacky vision of Carl Hiaasen, you need not wonder what's in store. But if you're new to this great author's literature, bless you. Be prepared to become a lifelong fan.

Five Hot 100 stars.

Cat Ellington's review of Kiss the Girls by James Patterson

My rating: 5 of 5 stars

Date read: January, 2003

The second literary feature to star psychologist and officer of the law, Alex Cross, *Kiss the Girls*—the psychological thriller succeeding its best-selling predecessor, *Along Came A Spider*—had ensnared and entertained my reader in no way less than that of its mind-blowing antecedent. By now, I am a true believer in the creative vision of the fiction's father, Patterson, and produce, before my fellow reader, yet another rave examination of his sophomore composition.

In mention of *Kiss the Girls*, the fast-paced and frigidly-suspenseful plot has our leading man, Cross, pitted against two notorious serial killers separately planted on both the East and West Coasts, via North Carolina: Casanova and the Gentleman Caller. The first of the two murderers, Casanova, is responsible for the murders of four people in 1975; and the other, the Gentleman Caller, brutally slaughtered a couple in 1981. Two homicidal maniacs, only one Alex Cross. Two homicidal maniacs, only one Scootchie Cross, beloved (and missing) niece of Alex Cross. Two homicidal maniacs, only one missing doctor, Kate McTiernan. Two homicidal maniacs, only three of the nation's coasts under a bloody siege. Two homicidal maniacs, only one James Patterson—a sensational scribbler of the MasterClass—who remains abreast of his ingenuity with an explosive dialogue of speed, grit, tenacity, sagacity, agitation, and one-step-ahead-of-you trepidation.

Kiss the Girls is a blessed work with true-to-form characters, all of whom would include big John Sampson - and a man of whom I strongly approve in every given way.

With an explosive conclusion you won't see coming, *Kiss the Girls* is well-penned magnificence. And those readers who love powerful psychological thrillers should consider James Patterson's *Kiss the Girls* highly recommended.

Five Cross-state stars.

Chapter 6
Above the Clouds of Confidence

Cat Ellington's review of Stormy Weather by Carl Hiaasen

My rating: 5 of 5 stars

Date read: March, 2003

I cannot even think about the name Carl Hiaasen without chuckling in response because he has that wonderfully distinctive and witty way of combining any number of serious social issues with just the right amount of hilarity. And it is for this reason that Carl Hiaasen has become one of my all-time favorite authors.

In *Stormy Weather*, yet another appreciable and gut-busting anecdote cleverly penned by the undisputed Master of the Crime Caper, the storyline blissfully circles around a pair of newlyweds (Max and Bonnie Lamb), a former Florida governor (the enigma, Skink), a female con artist partnered with an ex-con (Edie Marsh and Snapper), a mobile home salesman (Tony Torres), Tony's estranged wife (Neria Torres), a roaming wildlife farmer (Augustine Herrera), and a monkey – all of whom regrettably cross paths, either directly or indirectly, in the topsy-turvy aftermath of Hurricane Andrew.

Intertwined by way of insurance scams, street battles, government corruption, frenzied tourists, and a man-eating lion on the loose, this wacky ensemble exhibits a perfect rapport, bringing Hiaasen's incredible vision to vivid life over a non-stop pagination of 335. And to be frank, I was loath to witness the effort reach its end. For the dialogue had been just that enjoyable.

Stormy Weather is hands-down one sick and outrageous read. And I don't suspect that there is any authentic Carl Hiaasen devotee who would be inclined to disagree with me.

Five hurricane-ruptured stars.

Cat Ellington's review of Vanishing Act by Thomas Perry

My rating: 5 of 5 stars

Date read: March, 2003

Thrills. Chills. Suspense. Fear. Action. An exciting combination of ingredients eloquently added to the mystery-thriller gumbo that is Thomas Perry's admirably-composed fiction, *Vanishing Act*.

Vanishing Act is the first release in an entire series dedicated to its leading lady, the Native-American Jane Whitefield. Jane has a unique ability: she can help people—who don't want to be found by anyone—disappear.
Jane Whitefield is a one-woman Witness Protection Program, providing refuge to fugitives (most commonly those of questionable nature) in desperate search of new identities. And these would include a specific former cop named John Felker. Felker is on the run from an embezzlement charge, which Felker claims is a frame-up. And it won't be the first time that Jane has assisted the crooked in need: for she had also helped an old pal of John Felker, named Harry Kemple, vanish into thin air after his deceptive deeds were exposed. John Felker knows this. And he, too, wants to be evaporated into nothingness in an attempt to escape punishment for his self-inflicted ills.

Because Jane has made a spiritual pact with a mysterious tribe known as the Wolf Clan of the Seneca, she now has the power to elude hunters by assisting the hunted in the way of erasure. No matter what crimes they have committed and no matter who their pursuers are, Jane Whitefield can wipe out their former existence. And so far, she has done quite well in her lucrative business of creating new lives. That is until she decides to invent one for John Felker.

Vanishing Act was my exciting introduction to the literature of the gifted Thomas Perry. And in the wake of completing this thriller, I immediately became a new fan of his first-rate authorship. Not likely to disappoint any pundit of the mystery-thriller set, *Vanishing Act* is a delightful plot blessed with a swift pace and loads of on-the-edge-of-your-seat action. And readers are going to love it as the anecdote is jovially-commended and highly recommended.

Five evanescing stars.

Cat Ellington's review of It Had to Be You by Susan Elizabeth Phillips

My rating: 5 of 5 stars

Date read: June, 2003

Dearest reader,

I have just concluded my very first contemporary romance by Ms. Susan Elizabeth Phillips. And I must say that it was a love story to swoon over. Set in the beautiful city of Chicago, *It Had to Be You* is a romantic liaison about a lovely New Yorker named Phoebe Somerville that has come to the Windy City to claim her fascinating inheritance: the Chicago Stars professional football team. But, as one would expect, a woman—especially a beautiful woman—taking the reins of any entity established on the woodsy-scented rock of machismo is bound to have her hands full with the pride of men. And in Phoebe Somerville's case, such men just so happen to be professional athletes.

Lust and a battle for influential power control the very soul of this perfect effort as it orbits around the feminine succulence of Phoebe and the masculine bravado of the club's head coach, the fabled Dan Calebow. On the pages of *It Had to Be You*, Phoebe and Calebow come into play as adversaries - only to interlock in a passion so uncontrollably searing that the reader will need air-conditioning to keep cool while absorbing their wrangling, intimate and otherwise.

A gem in its respective class, Susan Elizabeth Phillips' *It Had to Be You* is a must-read for those adherents of the sexy romance genre. And I commend her authorship on a work well delivered, via both a spectacular setting and an enjoyable ensemble.

Five 50-yard line stars.

Cat Ellington's review of Dance for the Dead by Thomas Perry

My rating: 5 of 5 stars

Date read: September, 2003

Jane Whitefield is kickass!

Dance for the Dead is my second encounter with the top-billed star, and I am already in love, even wholeheartedly so, with her fearlessness and her no-nonsense disposition. Need a heart-thumping, nail-biting, and on-the-edge-of-your-seat mystery thriller to get you through a quiet and laid-back weekend? If so, then you might want to add Thomas Perry's masterful literary script, *Dance for the Dead*, to your "to-read" list.

Jane Whitefield (*Vanishing Act, Jane Whitefield, #1*) is back as a Senecan maven who specializes in the art of helping people in danger disappear. In *Dance for the Dead*, she travels cross-country to Los Angeles to assist a new customer named Timmy Phillips. Timmy is an eight-year-old trust fund baby wanted dead by those who avariciously covet his monetary properties - benefitted to him by his adoptive parents, both of whom, incidentally, have been brutally murdered in their home by professional killers.

Enter Mary Perkins. Mary is a desperate fugitive on the run for her thieving life after her involvement in a real-estate embezzlement scheme that defrauded millions of dollars out of some very high-profile banking institutions. The same hired killers are after Mary. And she pleads with Jane to help her escape the network of deadly hunters.

Jane, who was already preoccupied with her love life, eventually agrees to vanish the entire identity of Mary Perkins, proving just how good she is at the wipe-out. But is Jane Whitefield that good? Well, not according to the murderous firm blazing hot on Mary's trail. All in all, these barbarous individuals manage to stay one step ahead and not a single foot behind, especially not when millions of ill-gotten dollars have grown the wings of birds and hoisted themselves up in flight.

A must-read, fervently recommended, and Grishamesque in all of its apprehension, Thomas Perry's *Dance for the Dead* is an exceptional fiction in the mystery-thriller and suspense class. And to its indubitably adroit penman, I extend my sincerest kudos.

Five go on, take the money and run stars.

Cat Ellington's review of The Presence by John Saul

My rating: 4 of 5 stars

Date read: November, 2003

I'm one of those readers with cover love. I love book covers in much the same way that I do old album covers and movie posters. It's the art, you know? The colorful art. It mesmerizes me. And the moment I saw the cover art for John Saul's creepy sci-fi horror, *The Presence,* I knew I wanted to read the story that it so chillingly concealed.

The Presence is my introduction to John Saul. The tale presents a frightening, Hawaiian-set plot that revolves around Dr. Katherine Sundquist. Katherine is an anthropologist who specializes in African hominid research, the study of Man's evolution. As the storyline unfolds, Dr. Sundquist soon receives a job offer—via an ex-boyfriend—from an exclusive, albeit mysterious, research lab in Japan. The company would require Kat to travel to the beautiful Hawaiian island of Haleakala to concentrate her expertise on an unfamiliar set of skeletal remains that have been excavated right along the area of volcanic-lateral eruptions off the coast of Maui.
Kat is excited about the new job offer - not to mention the exotic locale where she will be doing her research. Before long, she gathers together her bags, her equipment, and her hesitant sixteen-year-old son, Michael, before taking off for the Pacific Coast on a new anthropological adventure. Or so she is misled to believe.

The scenery of the Hawaiian island, with its extravagant rainforest, is gorgeous, indeed. But what Dr. Katherine

Sundquist and her only child, the asthmatic Michael, don't yet realize is that they are about to ooh and aah themselves right through a darkened portal that leads downward - straight into the fiery depths of hell.

Yes, as Katherine's gut initially endeavored to warn her, the job offer was too good to be true.

Everything you ever thought you knew about the field of medicine comes to terrifying naught on the comparatively eerie pages of John Saul's *The Presence*. While not a five-star read, *The Presence* is still a dialogue that I would not hesitate to recommend to fans of sci-fi horror and suspense thrillers. The book was a fun read. And it would be the perfect anecdote with which to pass a lazy summer afternoon.

Happy reading, all.

Chapter 7
Beneath the Skies of Promise

Cat Ellington's review of The Picture of Dorian Gray by Oscar Wilde

My rating: 5 of 5 stars

Date read: February, 2004

"I have nothing to declare but my genius."
—Oscar Wilde

And indeed, the great man was just that, what a blatant genius. Regarding his masterwork of fiction currently under review, I read *The Picture of Dorian Gray* in 1983 after seeing *"The Sins of Dorian Gray,"* a made-for-TV movie released in that same year to debut on ABC. The film took its inspiration from Wilde's 1890 horror - in which a handsome nobleman named Dorian Gray sells his eternal soul to Satan in exchange for long-lasting youth. In the made-for-TV movie, an aspiring actress makes the same damning pact. Only she wants both physical beauty and the worldwide fame it will bring.

Before watching the fascinating film adaptation, I had never even heard of the classic fiction from which it took its inspiration. But the day after the film aired, I made my first acquaintance with the novel itself, compliments of the Chicago Public Library. And I loved it.

To this day, the very concept of the story's sinister dialogue still gives me the creeps: for *The Picture of Dorian Gray* is a narrative exposing the desperation of humankind, even a tale most petrifying. And it is not a composition easily forgotten in the wake of its conclusion.

Ever-reverberating and way ahead of its time, Oscar Wilde's *The Picture of Dorian Gray* has always been an unsurpassed cult classic in literature. And I reckon that it will continue to remain so for generations to come.

Five beauty is fleeting stars.

Cat Ellington's review of Absolute Power by David Baldacci

My rating: 5 of 5 stars

Date read: April, 2004

Question: Can the Commander-in-Chief commit murder and get away with it?

Billionaires, burglars, politicians, adultery, the Secret Service, and the act of voyeurism all butt heads - at breakneck speed - on the nail-biting pages of David Baldacci's political thriller, *Absolute Power*.

In the process of plundering the wealth of the super-rich, Luther Whitney, a well-seasoned thief working his trade in the nation's capital, becomes an eyewitness to cold-blooded murder. While hiding behind a two-way mirror in the master bedroom closet of a billionaire's home, he looks on to see the rich man's younger—and promiscuous—wife engaged in sexual relations with Alan Richmond, the very-inebriated President of the United States.
Lousy in bed, as the result of his drunkenness, Richmond soon becomes the target of malicious ridicule by the adulteress, Christine Sullivan. And the two undisclosed lovers begin to quarrel, physically. But what happens next leaves the would-be robber in a state of utter shock. Two members of the President's Secret Service detail would murder the billionaire's wife right before his very eyes after she wounds the Chief Executive with a letter opener in self-defense.

Suddenly sober and in cover-up mode, President Richmond contacts his Chief of Staff to dispose of the letter opener. But our leading man, Sticky Fingers Whitney, manages to escape the opulent premises with more vital evidence in his possession. Evidence that can undoubtedly bring down Richmond's entire presidency, as well as the political careers of those whose lives depend upon it. Even worse? The powers that be now know his identity. Even worse? There is now a tireless man-hunt underway to apprehend him dead or alive - but preferably dead.

A good novelist understands that vision, plot, pace, and a well-selected cast of players all make up a remarkable work of fiction. And David Baldacci's dexterous hand folds in and stirs together those main ingredients with expertise - as the dialogue of the heart-pounding *Absolute Power* so eloquently proves. An enjoyable political thriller that I would recommend to readers of John Grisham (*The Firm, 1991*) and Steve Martini (*Compelling Evidence, 1992*), *Absolute Power* kicks the door open for its author and could perhaps become one of the greatest political thrillers of all time.

Five presidential sealed stars.

Cat Ellington's review of The Last Juror by John Grisham

My rating: 4 of 5 stars

Date read: June, 2004

Although not among the most powerful (or fast-paced) of Grisham's legal thrillers, *The Last Juror* is still meritable of a satisfactory grade for integrity.

Set in the fictional town of Clanton, circa 1970, *The Last Juror* introduces Willie Traynor. Willie, a twenty-three-year-old college dropout, recently inherited *The Ford County Times* from its former owner after the dismal periodical became too unbearable to manage. Willie, who has a passion for journalism, secures a $50,000 loan from his affluent grandmother and buys the bankrupt publication, becoming its sole owner and editorial staff.

But *The Ford County Times*, under new management, barely has its printing presses up and running before a young mother and widow named Rhoda Kassellaw gets brutally murdered and raped in her quaint home. After an extensive investigation, Clanton authorities now have a suspect in custody. And that suspect? Danny Padgitt, a privileged member of one of the wealthiest and most influential families in the state.

Soon, the murder of Rhoda Kassellaw becomes the only talk of the town. The crime garners a bold-type headline in *The Times* as public opinion sways. And Danny Padgitt, who was pictured drenched in the dead woman's blood, meets his conviction and a possible death sentence that will depend upon a jury of his peers.

Enter our supporting lead, Ms. Callie Ruffin, an older Black woman and local of Clanton. Callie Ruffin is the proud mother of an extremely accomplished offspring of seven children, all doctors. And she becomes the first-ever African American to be featured in *The Ford County Times* as the result of her children's remarkable accomplishments, thanks to Willie Traynor. These two form a strong and loving bond of friendship with Ruffin in the process of researching her family for his periodical. Incidentally, Callie Ruffin is also the first (and only ever) African American selected to serve on a jury in the racially-wounded Mississippi haven of Ford County. The progress is groundbreaking, indeed. But not all are happy that an African American—in the state of Mississippi, no less—will be part of a jury that will decide whether or not a White man, a *rich* White man, should be sentenced to death for his capital punishment-worthy crimes.

Despite their newfound friendship, Callie and Willie are often bickering about the County's jury selection – at least they are over the many delicious meals that Callie prepares for her family and Willie. But what's worse is that Danny Padgitt has threatened to murder every single juror chosen to determine his miserable fate. And these would, of course, include the old Black woman who is Callie Ruffin. Yes, primarily her. Because an African American sending a Caucasian to his or her death in 1970s America could be considered no less than an abomination – by all Southern standards.

Regardless of its slower pace during certain scenes, *The Last Juror*, nevertheless, boasts a powerful historical message that exposes the blatantly wicked soul of the

South in decades bygone. Willie Traynor is flawless in his lead role as the first-person narrator of the anecdote, and Callie Ruffin shines in her capacity as the supporting lead. Lucien Wilbanks and Harry Rex Vonner, two prominent cast members from Grisham's bestselling *A Time to Kill*, also make cameo appearances in *The Last Juror.* The cross-referencing was a nice, little touch.

Overall, *The Last Juror* is an enjoyable and highly recommended read. But if you're one prone to fragile emotions, I would only advise that you be prepared to shed a tear or two, or maybe even three, as the storyline is one genuinely heavy in heart.

Happy reading, all.

Cat Ellington's review of Hoot by Carl Hiaasen

My rating: 4 of 5 stars

Date read: August, 2004

When big government money and land development are on the line, who gives a hoot about some silly ol' owl colony? Well, a bunch of determined school-age kids, that's hoo.

On the pages of this Newbery Award winner, the reader makes the acquaintance of its star, Roy Eberhardt, as he and his family settle into their new home state of Florida, particularly in its residential town of Coconut Cove. Like most children in his respective age group, Roy has attracted an awful bully in his fellow schoolmate Dana Matherson, a loathsome one to behold, even in the fictitious world of literature.

As the plot begins to unravel itself, Roy is off to his new school via school bus transport. He is then accosted by the irritable Dana, who has already selected the new kid to serve as his weaker punching bag. In an attempt to ignore the troublemaking Dana, Roy turns his face towards the window, where he then catches a glimpse of another young boy running barefoot along the sidewalk. And unable to remain at ease in the wake of this strange vision, Roy immediately gets up to vacate the school bus, that he may quickly follow in the running boy's direction. But he doesn't get far as Dana elects to block his departure and an unnecessary fight ensues.

While being strangled without cause by the self-loathing Dana Matherson, our Roy suddenly finds his courage. And with all of his inner strength, he hauls off and punches his aggressive bully smack dab in the nose, drawing rightful blood. But this courageous act of self-defense only ensures that Roy's dealings with the bullish Matherson are sure to get worse, and not better, as time swaggers forward.

Enter Napoleon Bridger "Mullet Fingers" Leep (say that five times fast). Napoleon is the barefoot runner Roy had been trying to catch up to before Dana picked his fight in the aisle of the big yellow school bus. Unbeknownst to Roy, Mullet Fingers had good reason to be running. He was running from the scene of his very own crime: vandalism of property. The property in question? A new building site for an upcoming dining franchise called Mother Paula's Pancake House. Pancakes, hotcakes, griddle cakes, flapjacks – no matter how you identify them, they're not welcome in these parts, mainly because of an endangered species of owl that nests on said site, namely the burrowing owl.

Napoleon Bridger "Mullet Fingers" Leep is on a mission to protect the endangered birds by doing everything in his power to prevent the pancake house from ever opening its doors in that location. That, or delaying its construction in any way he can. And after he finally meets and consults with Roy Eberhardt, the two misfit toys, er, boys, join forces to flip over the plans of the crooked, uncaring real estate developers, as well as the greedy, overtly corrupt politicians.

Here lies Carl Hiaasen's wacky creative vision. And if you know the written works of Carl Hiaasen, then you know that it's going to be one heck of a hilarious yarn.

Offset by a supporting cast of never-do-wells, Roy Eberhardt and Napoleon Bridger Leep render impressive performances in this Young Adult gem that tells the story of resolution and integrity. The courageous boys take a stance for the helpless and the hopeless, even in the hideous face of considerable opposition. Hiaasen's trademark humor is spread throughout, despite the narrative's somewhat plodding storyline. And though not a five-star composition by my reader's standard, Hoot still commands respect and is meritable.

Stand up for what you believe in, youngins. And happy reading, all.

Cat Ellington's review of The Gunslinger (The Dark Tower, #1) by Stephen King

My rating: 1 of 5 stars

Date read: October, 2004

My rating of the fantasy western currently under review does not in any way affect the immense love and respect that I will forever foster for its authorship.

The first in King's *The Dark Tower* series, *The Gunslinger* orbits around a gunfighter named Roland Deschain, a man on a desert mission to find the so-called "man in black," believed to be the otherworldly Randall Flagg, his eternal nemesis. If memory serves you correctly, dear reader, you will know that Randall Flagg made his antagonistic debut in King's 823-page epic, *The Stand*, ca. 1978. Driven by a fierce desire to face-off with his elusive adversary, Roland treks through the bone-dry heat of a vast desert in his search. On the course of his journey, Roland interacts with other players in the series, including his makeshift son, the mysterious Jake Chambers; Alice of Tull, a bar owner who may or may not have information on the whereabouts of the man in black; Sylvia Pittston, the pregnant clergywoman; Cuthbert Allgood, a free-spirited gunslinger; and farmer Brown. By the way, farmer Brown is the owner of Zoltan, the black crow.

These top-billed cast members are only a small segment of an even larger ensemble that accounts for the five-part fictional series. The collection is timeless, according to some. But for me, *The Gunslinger (The Dark Tower, #1)* failed to be enticing. And it could be because westerns and

fantasy fiction do not wow me as much as raw horror –
with which the great Stephen King is so synonymous.

While I commend King for his literary prolificacy, I do not,
however, extol *The Gunslinger*. I understood the spiritual
overtones of the fiction's premise, sure, but even still, the
same is not one of the great man's most phenomenal
efforts.

For those diehard devotees of western fiction and fantasy
fiction—mingled with just a half teaspoon of horror—*The
Gunslinger* comes highly recommended by me for your
reading pleasure. Unfortunately, the plot had nothing more
that it could do to fulfill my own.

Happy reading, folks.

Cat Ellington's review of Sole Survivor by Dean Koontz

My rating: 3 of 5 stars

Date read: December, 2004

Some readers will say that *Sole Survivor* is a mystery novel, while other readers will label the work a suspense thriller. And both are right, save for their missing one key element, that being "conspiracy." Indeed, said anecdote is not anything short of a conspiracy thriller. Plain and simple. The entire premise of this literary composition, scribbled by the legendary Dean Koontz, screams conspiracy thriller, even more so than it does "mystery thriller" or "suspense thriller." There are components of mystery and suspense, sure, and the plot is undoubtedly thriller fiction, but it is thriller fiction that leans more towards its subgenre of conspiracy fiction. And with that, boys and girls, my brief examination of this effort will now proceed.

Joe Carpenter, the star of *Sole Survivor*, is a man living a life of grief and regret. Only one year earlier, Carpenter sadly lost his wife and their two daughters to a tragic plane crash that claimed the lives of all but one: a woman named Rose Tucker.
Now approaching the first anniversary of the catastrophic event, Joe and Rose meet by "coincidence," and she begins to witness to him that she survived the fiery crash, which is questionable, considering that there were no survivors at the time of the wreck. Naturally, Joe Carpenter doesn't immediately buy what the conundrum woman is selling, and Rose knows this; nevertheless, she goes on, working to convince the widower by continuing to provide

him with only a limited supply of information until she can win him over. Joe Carpenter, now fired up with righteous indignation about the senseless loss of his family, begins to seek out the truth about what caused that plane to descend from the darkened sky on that fateful evening. But what Joe Carpenter really should have done was just left well enough alone.

Who is this woman, Rose Tucker? And from whence has she come? What dark and dangerous secrets is she harboring? Who is the billionaire named Horton Nellor? And what on earth is Teknologik, Inc.? Who wants Joe Carpenter dead now that he knows too much?
These questions and more are what place Dean Koontz's *Sole Survivor* in the arena of a mystery. But is it the dark trepidation of the storyline that makes it a suspense thriller? Do the sinister activities of corporate entities add the conspiracy factor?

Generally speaking, *Sole Survivor* is a good read, but not a great one. With the dialogue, Koontz presents a well-balanced script and employs a fairly decent cast. But the two could not keep up with one another. And that resulted in a slower pace and ho-hum reading experience. Still, what I may regard as sedate, another will not. And for this reason, I am inclined to recommend *Sole Survivor* to those of you thriller buffs in the literary community so that you may first consume the narrative and then go about drawing your conclusions henceforth.

Enjoy.

Chapter 8
Within the Dense Forests of Opposition

Cat Ellington's review of The Mist by Stephen King

My rating: 5 of 5 stars

Date read: February, 2005

Quite spooky, indeed, as has come to be expected from the great Master of Horror. If I may say as much, just the premise of Stephen King's *The Mist* will give you goosebumps.

The day after a fierce thunderstorm, a heavy, abnormal mist is left in its wake, fully encompassing Bridgton, a small town in the coastal state of Maine. Opaque enough to obstruct visibility, this misty fog serves as a cover for those who do not belong here in this three-dimensional physical realm. For the horrifying and otherworldly legion have arrived. And power has been given to them to sting and obliterate. For the rulers of the darkness of this age have come prepared: for they have come to launch a vicious and murderous attack on any human being that dares to venture out of doors, or, in this case, out from behind the four walls of a town supermarket – inside of which several humans remain stationed for safety's sake.

I dared to read *The Mist* late into the evening, right before retiring to bed. And I would not advise that any other reader do the same.

Starring David Drayton, Billy Drayton, and Amanda Dumfries, *The Mist* is yet another favorite from the extensive and storied collection of the inimitable Stephen King. A short, albeit exceptionally-written, horror, *The Mist* is sure to terrify its readers of thunderstorms, infusing in the same a dreadful fear of what they might leave behind, save clean, fresh air.

Five profoundly horrifying stars.

Cat Ellington's review of A Painted House by John Grisham

My rating: 2 of 5 stars

Date read: March, 2005

Were his name not credited as this fiction's author, one would not believe that John Grisham penned *A Painted House*.

A Painted House, a book inspired by his childhood years in Arkansas, had its moments, yes. But even still, the effort was overall one of the slowest and intellectually aggravating storylines that I have ever read. And that's putting it kindly. Concerning his work here, John Grisham's *A Painted House* was a challenging read for me. Not because it was so emotional that I could not stop the tears from flowing, but because the work was so atrociously plodding, moving along at a pace that I would personally liken to the flow of molasses.

Grisham's dialogue, set in 1950s Arkansas, is given grace by way of the very articulate, first-person narration of Luke Chandler, the seven-year-old protagonist with whom I fell madly in love. Luke Chandler tells the reader about the rough life he lives with his parents and grandparents on a cotton farm in the South. Young Luke toils daily, in the cotton fields, together with two generations of men come before him: his father Jesse, and his grandfather, Pappy.

The plot begins to thicken like country gravy when Pappy Chandler takes little Luke along with him to the market square in search of migrant workers to assist the Chandler clan with work on their farm - mainly in the service of picking cotton. And while looking over several employable prospects, the elder Pappy and young Luke meet and greet a family of so-called "hill people," as in "hillbillies," and immediately hire them. The family is named Spruill. And the Chandlers, considering themselves fortunate to have found such an enthusiastic bunch of folks to assist them with the back-breaking farm labor, even offer the family Spruill room and board on their property as a convenience. The deal couldn't be better, and the Spruill family accepts. In the beginning, the arrangement would *seem* harmonious enough. But in due time, it would slowly reveal its true spirit of envy, jealousy, covetousness, and bitterness.

Hank Spruill, the violent and mentally unstable eldest child of Mr. and Mrs. Spruill, eventually comes undone, and the shattering chain of events that soon follow will forever alter the close-knit Chandlers and everything they ever held dear.

For John Grisham, *A Painted House* is a 180-degree turn from his standard legal thrillers – a class in which he reigns, comfortably; but just composing my examination of this anecdote brought upon my psyche fatigue unexplainable, save for the fact that the witness was only too unhurried. Is the script itself interesting enough to merit my recommendation? Yes, it most certainly is, but only if the potential reader doesn't mind a slower motion in the page-turning process.

Happy reading, all.

Cat Ellington's review of The Judge (Paul Madriani, #4) by Steve Martini

My rating: 5 of 5 stars

Date read: May, 2005

When it comes to the literature of Steve Martini, where the leading man of his political and legal thrillers is concerned, I pretty much walked into his fictional world out of sync. Case in point: *The Judge*, book #4 in the Paul Madriani series, and my introduction to his authorship. *Trader of Secrets*, book #12 in the Paul Madriani series, would be my second Martini effort. Out of order much? Yes, but there is no need to dwell upon it.

"Judge not, that you be not judged."
—Matthew 7:1

The quoted Scripture is not towards you, dear reader, but rather, the quoted Scripture is to set the mood for my examination of the narrative currently under critique.

Set in the state of California, Steve Martini's *The Judge* rotates around Armando Acosta, a justice of the court apprehended for solicitation of sexual relations with a woman whom he, at the outset, believed to be a working girl for sale. But suspicious is justice Acosta's sudden arrest, given that the passionately-hated jurist is also overseeing a case involving an alleged murder cover-up by law enforcement officials.

"Coconuts," as Justice Acosta is so maliciously-dubbed, has become a thorn in the side of not only the Chief of

Police but the entire department-at-large. And someone wants the tyrannical judge out of the way. But who?

Enter our leading man, Paul Madriani. Madriani is a respected defense attorney with whom Justice Acosta has often quarreled, if only verbally. But despite their butting heads in Acosta's courtroom, nevertheless, Paul Madriani is the only one on whom Judge Armando Acosta can depend. He used to rely on his first defense attorney, Lenore Goya, but he no longer does. Because he removed her from the case. Why? Because investigators found her fingerprints at the murder scene. To make matters worse, the now humbled Acosta has to accept the reality that all of his professional peers have turned their backs on him.

Paul reluctantly agrees to defend the judge out of some sympathetic sense of moral obligation. But his case bearing the name of the now-infamous Armando Acosta is going to be an uphill climb - especially now that Coleman Kline, the pit bull of all DAs, has decided to prosecute the disgraced Acosta to the fullest extent of the law. And DA Coleman Kline is taking no prisoners, but many names.

There are stumbling blocks aplenty on the pages of this exceptional legal thriller, but even still, these few questions remain: Did the judge do what was evil, or didn't he? And if he did not, then who did? Who fosters so much loathing for Judge Armando Acosta that he or she only wishes to see his prominent life utterly destroyed? Who is trying to frame a Capital County Justice for murder? And will our top-billed star, the beloved and respected Paul Madriani, be able to salvage what's left of the judge's honor?

The answers to those questions (and more) reveal themselves wondrously on these rapidly-paced pages of high-octane legal suspense. Steve Martini—a former journalist and attorney himself—completely wowed me with his skillful dialogue and outstanding cast selection in *The Judge*. And in the wake of concluding the fiction, he can now claim a new admirer in me. I enjoyed *The Judge* wholeheartedly—despite being on my sickbed while reading it (common cold be damned)—and I would indeed rule in favor of its loftiest recommendation.

Five gavel-banging stars.

Cat Ellington's review of Trader of Secrets (Paul Madriani, #12) by Steve Martini

My rating: 3 of 5 stars

Date read: July, 2005

I liked Paul Madriani so much in Steve Martini's *The Judge* (my introduction to the author's literature) that I could hardly wait to read *Trader of Secrets*, the twelfth in a legal thriller series starring the defense attorney. And while the plot was *somewhat* entertaining, it neglected to blow away the psyche of my legal-thriller-loving reader in the same way that *The Judge* had. Still, *Trader of Secrets* is one of those narratives that many readers will either love, hate, or moderately admire. I just so happen to be included among the latter.

The setback here is that while the dialogue possessed a good enough grip to hold my interest until the very end, there were too many characters on these pages. And when there are too many characters, there is confusion. Or at least an induction of aggravation. If I may say as much, I got the feeling that Martini had something to prove with this effort. And perhaps he did, considering that *Trader of Secrets* is his third work featuring Muerte Liquida, an either truly ruthless or just plain idiotic, Mexican assassin hell-bent on revenge. Liquida wants Paul Madriani dead. And he would abolish the Esquire for good was it not for so many other obstacles laid out to prevent him from doing so.

Let's see, there's Paul's partner and good friend Herman Diggs, who, by the way, has been viciously attacked by Liquida and left for dead. And then there's Harry Hinds, another close pal of Madriani's, after whom the angry assassin seeks - to murder him, too. There is also the lovely Joselyn Cole, Madriani's girlfriend, mind you, who would be a tasty kill, indeed, and a perfect tool for the assassin to use against his adversary. Paul's daughter, Sarah, and her Doberman, Bugsy, are not exempt from the murderous Liquida's crosshairs, either. And, dare I say it, Liquida's grocery, uh, vengeance list goes on to include members of NASA personnel who are involved in traitorous oil dealings with America's most heinous enemy after Russia: The Middle East.

For a dangerous and well-trained assassin, it is taking Muerte Liquida a long time to snub out his prey, Paul Madriani, even into this, the third narrative to showcase the warring pair. Assassins assassinate. But for some strange reason or another, Muerte Liquida cannot bring Paul Madriani to naught. Is Madriani that clever, even enough to continuously slip through the hands of this enraged killer? I'll let you, dear reader, be the judge of that.
And speaking of judgment, with *Trader of Secrets* being only my second Steve Martini reading experience, I am not really at liberty to be more comprehensive in my critique of the writer's range. But I will admit that *The Judge* was irrefutably fascinating. And because of it, I developed a desire to venture further into the literature of its authorship.

Trader of Secrets is in no way a terrible read. It's just not as fast-paced in its storyline and plot as *The Judge* had been - at least not by my legal thriller-affectionate standards. Even still, I would recommend *Trader of Secrets* to any singular devotee of this legendary class. And I do intend to carry on in my pursuit of the Steve

Martini novel, as his writing style is reminiscent of that belonging to my dearly beloved John Grisham.

Have fun.

Cat Ellington's review of Velocity by Dean Koontz

My rating: 5 of 5 stars

Date read: December, 2005

He feels the need, the need for speed.

And *Velocity*, the terrifying suspense thriller penned by Dean Koontz, one of my all-time favorite authors in the genres of horror and suspense, is sure to command its reader just that, what speed in his or her reading.

In this fast-paced - pun intended - masterwork, the breathless plot orbits around an introverted writer named Billy Wiles. Billy has pretty much become a hermit-like recluse since his beloved wife fell into a coma only a few years before. Billy now lives a low-key existence, working as a bartender to help make ends meet. And as far as friends are concerned, Billy Wiles can name only a few; he doesn't have a social life. Yes, this is the settled reality for Billy Wiles: quiet and rather average. That is, until the day he discovers the chilling note laid neatly on the windshield of his car. The message was composed by an author who gives our easy-going leading man a paralyzing ultimatum: 'If you don't take this note to the police . . . I will kill a lovely blond schoolteacher. If you do, I will kill an elderly woman active in charity work.' Believing the chilling note to be nothing more than a sick prank, Billy disregards it. Until a blond schoolteacher is found brutally murdered, and Billy receives a second note.

Dean Koontz's *Velocity* is the sort of heart-pounding suspense that its viewer will find quite challenging to cast aside, even if for a little while. Extremely well-written in graphic detail, the storyline unfurls before the very eye in a dreadful spirit of trepidation, transporting the reader on an anxiety-fueled rollercoaster ride that gradually climbs to a remarkably high peak before plunging the same downward into the steep depths of unadulterated fear.

A master of his craft, Koontz neglects to disappoint, presenting before his fandom a flawless script graced by the eloquence of a tour de force cast - and a few cameo quotes from the one and only T.S. Eliot. Evidently recommended, and buoyantly so, *Velocity* is an adrenaline rush of perfection for those suspense-thriller enthusiasts who harbor insatiable desires for all things thrills, chills, and blood spilled.

Five gasping stars.

Chapter 9
Into A New Era

Cat Ellington's review of Fine Beauty by Sam Fine

My rating: 5 of 5 stars

Revised analysis: June, 2006

A joy and a blessing to my beauty buff had been this precious jewel of nonfiction, composed by one of the greatest cosmeticians known to Mankind. Yes, Sam Fine. I first read *Fine Beauty* in the early winter of 1999, not long after its initial release. And though I'd composed a detailed review of the reference in the wake of completing it at that time, until now, I was still unable to locate the analysis – despite my extensive search efforts. Therefore, I have concluded that I had perhaps stored it away with a small batch of other reviews missing from my collection in my second city of residence. That or the examination is lost forever.

So, for the sake of rendering to this fine and direly recommended composition the exuberant recognition it so richly deserves, I will say this: Sam Fine's *Fine Beauty* is a most exceptional beauty to behold.

On these delightful, glossy pages, Fine creates his marvelous art on the washed canvases of some of the world's most stunning women, including Naomi Campbell, Tyra Banks, Iman, Veronica Webb, and Vanessa L. Williams, to name a few. And the lovely reference would serve as the ideal go-to for any woman possessing an interest in the artistry of cosmetic application – begotten by the phenomenal philosophy of aesthetics. I love Sam Fine. And I love his greatly-blessed creativity on fine display here.

Five perfectly arched stars.

Cat Ellington's review of Swan by Naomi Campbell

My rating: 5 of 5 stars

Revised analysis: July, 2006

Much like the examination that had been composed by me for the prior effort, the original review that I'd written for Naomi Campbell's *Swan* has become a challenge for me to locate today. But the first time I viewed the nonfiction—detailing the world-famous supermodel's rise to unprecedented fame in the fashion industry—was back in late 1999, not long after I'd completed Sam Fine's *Fine Beauty*. On the pages of this intriguing read, Campbell exposes any number of evil trials that pursue those women of African descent, respectively, in the opulent world of high fashion, including the ugliest one of them all: racism. Not shocking but disdainful.

Campbell testifies about her many unhappy experiences in the fashion industry that stemmed from racism. And not only her but also other Black models. If it had not been the natural texture of her hair being mocked and ridiculed, then it had been her lips (gloriously luscious and genuinely beautiful as they are), or the shape of her nose, or the rich shade of her complexion. Here lies the towering beauty's heartfelt witness, tried and true. She is Naomi Campbell. One of many who is God-created but judged and hated in this present world.
And there are more than a few women who will relate to this witness.

Determination is the dominant factor on these pages as the effort's leading lady takes her readers away to some of the most exotic places in the world on her quest to make it big in fashion. And boy, did she ever. Naomi takes the expertly stitched and well-heeled jet-set of haute couture and many a Fashion Week by storm with her merciless runway strut and her irrefutable ability to love the camera just as much as it does her. Naomi Campbell is a rarity in her class, a uniquely designed piece of the fashion community's puzzle. And I love her.

Kudos to the woman who exudes confidence, even in the scornful faces of racial hatred and envious adversity. Because if she does not believe in herself, then who in the hell else will? Naomi Campbell's *Swan*. Exuberantly commended and jauntily recommended.

Five Vogue-Elle-and Mademoiselle-worthy stars.

Cat Ellington's review of Spectacular Chicago by Thomas B. Allen

My rating: 5 of 5 stars

Date read: October, 2006

My, oh my! That joyful expression results from my reading Thomas B. Allen's *Spectacular Chicago*, which perhaps is one of the most gorgeously arrayed and informative references in its respective genre: for the coffee table book is a must-have!

Spectacular Chicago has vast knowledge and pays homage to the most beautiful city in the world. This pleasantly colorful hardcover edition features in-depth facts about both the city's native and immigrant inhabitants. It also features architecture designed and constructed by several gentlemen renowned for their masterworks in architectural science. These include Frank Lloyd Wright, Louis Sullivan, William Drummond, Daniel Burnham, John Wellborn Root, William Holabird, and Martin Roche, to name a few.

There's even an exciting layout detailing the city's magnificent parks, landmark districts, and its one-and-only museum campus – not to be outdone by many diverse neighborhoods (77 to be exact), restaurant, recreation centers, and yes, that glorious ol' Lakefront, draped in a beautiful shade of emerald green and sparkling a vivid hue of vibrant blue to the far East Side of them all.

Guaranteed to keep its reader absorbed for hours, Thomas B. Allen's *Spectacular Chicago* has a little bit of something for everyone, from the aboriginal to the tourist alike. And if I do say so myself, the edition is a radiant gem worth owning and sharing in the company of friends and family as it makes for an excellent conversational piece. Congratulations on a job well done, Thomas B. Allen.

Five picturesque stars.

Cat Ellington's review of The Boondocks: Because I Know You Don't Read the Newspaper by Aaron McGruder

My rating: 5 of 5 stars

Date read: December, 2006

Political correctness be damned!

The Boondocks: Because I Know You Don't Read the Newspaper (The Boondocks #1) is nothing less than what we have come to expect from one of the most undisputed names in comic books, the same being Aaron McGruder.

It had been in the final year of the 20th century (1999) that the now internationally recognized cartoonist launched into the realm of fame with his internationally recognized comic strip, *The Boondocks*, via Universal Press Syndication. The truth-bearing comic strip, which dances a Jig around the lives of two young brothers (biologically- and racially-speaking) named Huey and Riley Freeman pioneered an entirely new method of storytelling in the entertaining world of comic strips. Blessed with a unique vision, McGruder brought change—in harmony with the African American experience—through the visual arts. He managed to rebuke every fiber in the wretched being of the so-called Status Quo by exposing the hideousness of systematic racism, societal oppression, fear, Black-on-Black warfare, and the soul deteriorating spirit called self-hatred. For in the evil world system, every man and every woman should know his and her place. Because should he or she not know his or her place in society, how on earth could the system (or the "Matrix," if you will) suffice to maintain its operation?

The raw, loathsome, and viciously brutal truth, saturated in a dose of side-splitting humor, is what the ingenuine McGruder admirably relays to his cult followers, one ire-inducing strip at a time.

On the pages of *The Boondocks: Because I Know You Don't Read the Newspaper*, Huey and Riley suddenly find themselves uprooted from Chicago's jet-Black South Side only to relocate to the lily-White suburb of Woodcrest, where the two boys go to dwell with their Granddad, Robert Freeman. The move is a shock to both boys, who refer to their new neighborhood as the 'Boondocks.'

Huey and Riley, both pro-Black, don't necessarily care for their new neighbors of the Caucasian persuasion either. And the boys make it priority number one to verbally inform the same of as much, in no uncertain terms.

Funny, thought-provoking, educational, keen on self-awareness, and racially-charged, *The Boondocks: Because I Know You Don't Read the Newspaper (The Boondocks #1)* is the tour de force comic strip collection that started it all for Aaron McGruder. The strip also inspired a syndicated show on *Adult Swim*, a Cartoon Network programming block that ran from 2005 - 2014, garnering 55 masterful episodes.

Added to this satirical narrative is a powerful foreword, penned by the Hip-Hop activist and self-proclaimed Media Assassin, Harry Allen, the pride and joy of Harlem, New York.

Since its debut in the *Chicago Sun-Times*, I have considered myself a die-hard fan of McGruder's first-rate comic strip series, *The Boondocks*. And there isn't a doubt in my mind that anyone new to *The Boondocks*—be it in book form or as an animated sitcom—will also become one, even if only progressively: for the stratospherically recommended *The Boondocks* is, in itself, an acquired taste.

Five militant stars.

Cat Ellington's review of Natural Born Charmer by Susan Elizabeth Phillips

My rating: 5 of 5 stars

Date read: April, 2007

Life is but a dream. . .

Natural Born Charmer is a romantic and fun-filled tale about a rich, famous, and ridiculously handsome professional football quarterback who falls madly in love with an all-around average gal.

Meet Dean Robillard. Dean is the superstar Chicago Stars quarterback riding the statuesque waves of mega fame - not only on the roster of a professional football club but also in his lucrative second career as a drool-worthy billboard model for EndZone, a factory sports underwear manufacturer. The world is indeed Dean Robillard's oyster, and he takes his precious time enjoying all that his life has to offer. Even behind the wheel of his ultra-expensive sports car, the most eligible bachelor in America rules the wide-and-spacious roads of Chicago. That is until he finally hits a proverbial bump in one of them, or rather, alongside one of them.

Unable to believe his bedroom eyes, the tall and solidly built star quarterback beholds a beaver walking about the roadside. But this beaver is not your ordinary, paddle-tailed, buck-toothed, and clumsy-mumsy forest rodent. Oh no, this particular beaver just so happens to be a mascot costume worn by a very irritated and furious young woman who has just been duped and left stranded - out in the middle of nowhere.

Enter our leading lady, Blue Bailey, a woman on a determined mission to murder her despicable ex-boyfriend, or to at least beat the living crap out of him. For Blue is a woman way past scorned. Our Blue is a woman who has had enough of all the miserable crap that life has thus far shoved down her throat. For Blue is a woman whose feet are right at the cold threshold of her own wit's end. And she's just about to fully cross it when she spots the sleek and shiny black sports car slowly pulling up alongside her. The handsome driver greets her, but she refuses to return any chit-chat. See, unbeknownst to our Blue Bailey, the sexy stranger behind the wheel is none other than Chicago Stars quarterback Dean Robillard – whom, thank heavens, is persistent.

Finally bringing her brisk walk to a slower stroll, by way of some small talk and a few annoying jokes regarding the hot and sticky beaver costume, Dean Robillard offers Blue Bailey a ride, and she eventually accepts.

It would be the best decision our beloved Blue has ever made.

From that moment on, the plot only thickens to a much better texture, adding in a pinch of humor and one whole clove of excitement. Susan Elizabeth Phillips outdoes herself with this mesmerizing effort! The author employs an unforgettable ensemble of supporting players whose own characters make this fast-paced romantic comedy even more of a delight to read: an aging rock star, a fiftyish former rock and roll groupie, a darling eleven-year-old girl who turns out to be Dean Robillard's long-lost relative, and an old, embittered woman resolved to become an excruciating thorn in the side of them all.

Natural Born Charmer is a perfect read, regardless of the season. The effort has style, poise, character, soul, and an endearing personality that commands love, respect, and above all, a jaunty recommendation. I loved, loved, loved this novel of romance! And I was loath to complete it with the turning of the final page: for I regretted parting ways with such a tremendous script and cast. And so will you, too, my fellow reader. What a glorious read.

Five hut-hut-hike stars.

Cat Ellington's review of Star Island by Carl Hiaasen

My rating: 5 of 5 stars

Date read: July, 2010

"Tastes so good make a grown man cry, sweet cherry pie."
—Warrant

After reading a slow and tedious work of fiction before it, *Star Island*—penned by the great Carl Hiaasen—served as a sort of minty antiseptic that worked wonders for my reader's palate – washing away the wretched aftertaste that lingered in the wake of my concluding it.

Hiaasen's title, *Star Island*, takes its name from Star Island in Miami Beach, the hot, sticky, and ultra-rich setting for yet another one of the author's outrageously wacky and unputdownable crime capers. On the pages of this craftily-written tale, the reader is provided with an up-close and personal view into the skin-crawling lifestyles of an annoying - and often brutal - cast of players who have their calloused feet planted in show business: Popstars, managers, agents, bodyguards, and actors; and in the media: the Paparazzi and the tabloids. These are those who take center stage, each one rendering a literary award-worthy performance and doing their massively endeared creator a phenomenal justice in turn.
The *Star Island* plot wraps itself around Cheryl Bunterman, a twenty-two-year-old Pop music star better known by her world-famous stage name, Cherry Pye. A sensation in the music industry, the alcoholic and drug-addicted Cherry Pye's career is under the management of her mother, Janet Bunterman, and her finances (considerable as they

are) are overseen by her greedy, controlling, and conniving father, Ned Bunterman.

As the non-stop action gets underway, we head into the cozy confines of an all-exclusive, five-star hotel in South Beach, where our ever-popular Pop-tart, Cherry, is laid out flat from another drug-induced overdose. Enter Ann Delusia, an aspiring actress and the spitting image of Cherry Pye. Ann, hired by Cherry's parents as the star's body double whenever Cherry is too incapacitated to make public appearances, plays her part well on these pages. And once again, her professional services are desperately required under the hectic circumstances. The deceptive game always goes according to plan, and no one ever suspects a thing. But Cherry's lucky streak begins to near its end when Claude "Bang" Abbott, a morbidly obese paparazzo—who just so happens to harbor an unhealthy obsession with the Pop diva—determines that something is not quite right about *his* Cherry Pye on the evening in question: *Yeah, she looks like Cherry, but she ain't Cherry,* so the big Bang Abbott thinks. And if this broad ain't Cherry Pye, then who in the hell is she?
Leave it to a lonely and bloated ol' paparazzo—who'll do just about anything to win the superstar singer's attention and affections—to dig down to the bottom of the mystery. He'll even involve the tabloids. Yes, crazy is as crazy does. And with Carl Hiaasen's outrageous vision guiding the thigh-slapping plot along, things get downright scandalous and vile.

Adding to an already memorable company of top-billed literary genius are the following:

- Maury Lykes is the depraved pedophile who is also the record promoter for Cherry Pye. He's a real me, myself, and I kind of guy.

- Tanner Dane Keefe is a good-looking young actor and Cherry Pye's love interest. Much like Cherry, Tanner Dane Keefe is immune to real talent – his only claim to fleeting fame being his placement in an upcoming Quentin Tarantino satirical flick.

- Lila and Lucy Lark are the inseparable fraternal twins and Cherry Pye's chain-smoking publicists. Mistresses of their remarkable (joint) trade—where cleaning up the messes of spoiled and self-destructive stars in the entertainment industry are concerned—the twin sisters Lark are forever in great demand. But they remain restricted to only the most distinguished of A-list celebrities.

- Blondell Wayne "Chemo" Tatum is a hideously disfigured felon first introduced in Hiaasen's uproarious masterpiece, *Skin Tight*. Chemo—whose amputated arm now wields a deadly weed wacker—is soon hired to serve as the foolish and annoying Cherry Pye's bodyguard. And Blondell Wayne "Chemo" Tatum is not one who suffers fools (or the annoying) gladly.

With cameo appearances by Clinton "Skink" Tyree and Jim Tile, among a talented troupe of additional supporting players, Carl Hiaasen's exorbitantly recommended *Star Island* is a heavenly body of literature perfectly fit for the crime caper record books. No doubt, any given number of frivolous "Poptarts" in the music industry will solemnly swear on her individual (and extremely short-lived) career that she alone inspired this timeless work of superior fiction.

Five spoiled rotten-talentless-and-entitled stars.

Coming August 2019

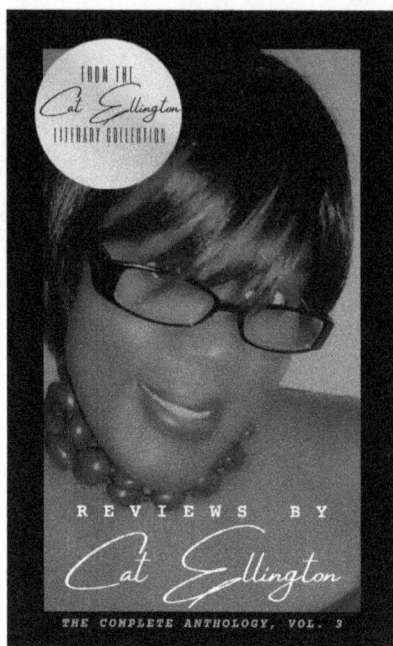

Reviews by Cat Ellington: The Complete Anthology, Vol. 3
Imprint: Quill Pen Ink Publishing
Cover Hue: Bubblegum Yum

About the Author

Cat Ellington is an American songwriter, casting director, poet, author, and businesswoman from Chicago, IL. She is best known for her creative contributions to the diverse industries and fields of music, movies, art, and literature.

Outside of her professional element, the award-winning creative enjoys reading, listening to music, cooking, collecting vintage and modern charm bracelets, watching movies and classic TV shows, sailing, jet-skiing, playing tennis, and eating frozen yogurt -- lots of it.

Cat Ellington on Amazon: Books, Biography, Blog, Audiobooks, Kindle

Cat Ellington at the Award-Winning Boutique Domain

Cat Ellington at The Review Period with Cat Ellington

Cat Ellington at IMDb

<u>Cat Ellington at Goodreads</u>

**The following is a preview of Reviews by Cat
Ellington: The Complete Anthology, Vol. 3**

FROM THE
Cat Ellington
LITERARY COLLECTION

R E V I E W S   B Y

Cat Ellington

THE COMPLETE ANTHOLOGY, VOL. 3

Reviews by Cat Ellington

Books by Cat Ellington

REVIEWS BY CAT ELLINGTON: THE COMPLETE
ANTHOLOGY, VOL. 1

REVIEWS BY CAT ELLINGTON: THE COMPLETE
ANTHOLOGY, VOL. 2

THE MAKING OF DUAL MANIA: FILMMAKING
CHICAGO STYLE

REVIEWS BY CAT ELLINGTON – THE COMPLETE
ANTHOLOGY LIMITED EDITION HOLIDAY GIFT SET
(BOOKS 1 & 2)

REVIEWS BY CAT ELLINGTON: THE COMPLETE
ANTHOLOGY, VOL. 3

Reviews by Cat Ellington
The Complete Anthology, Vol. 3

Cat Ellington

Quill Pen Ink Publishing

THE BEAUTY OF EXPRESSION™

CHICAGO

PAPERBACK ISBN: 978-1-7334421-0-7
HARDCOVER ISBN: 978-1-7370971-7-4

Library of Congress Control Number: 2022362727

Cover design: Hues of the Reviews
Vol. 3 Hue: Bubblegum Yum
The Cat Ellington Literary Collection

Published by Quill Pen Ink Publishing
Chicago, Illinois, USA
https://quill-pen-ink-publishing.business.site/

Quill Pen Ink Publishing, 2019

Hardcover Edition: October 2021

Printed in the U.S.A.

Dedication

To Judy Mui—
Golden Gate princess, special friend,
and the grooviest China girl in all the world

Foreword

Those of us who have not only a love of reading but also a deep affection (and respect) for the written word know far too well that the craft can at times be both exhilarating and challenging. It all depends upon what day a writer happens to run into some mental roadblocks. But then there are also times when one happens upon a writer whose clarity of insight, along with their indescribable gift of observation into human nature, causes us to see things and people differently.

Case in point: Cat Ellington. It is through such a lens that Cat Ellington is perceived. I have known her for quite some time and am thoroughly familiar with her work as a versatile songwriter/composer, poet, author, and film casting director. But when Cat began to convey to me - many years ago - that she had been creating book reviews since the (tender) age of eleven, I was speechless - because I hadn't expected that literary criticism was among her many extraordinary talents in the arts.

While I am immensely impressed by her (adroit) insight and her bawdy sense of humor, what I genuinely admire about the Cat Ellington review is the nurturing and empathetic outlook that it presents. It says a lot about its author and her exceptional ability to understand - through great spiritual wisdom - the deepest (and sometimes darkest) innermost workings of Mankind - by way of the human body, and the human mind, and the human soul. This quality is what sets Cat Ellington apart from all the rest. What also makes the Cat Ellington review so unique is the way she incorporates a vast spectrum of references for each critique, including Biblical scriptures, movies, television shows, and music. This method is her way of highlighting key points in both plot and character.

That said, I will encourage all of you readers to buckle up and have fun because you're in for the word-slingin' ride of your life - as only Cat Ellington can navigate it.

Joseph Strickland

Writer/Director

Preface

Hello again, my dearest readers. It has been exactly one year since the release of *Reviews by Cat Ellington: The Complete Anthology, Vol. 1.* And in the time since, we've proudly published two more books in the progressive series, including *Reviews by Cat Ellington: The Complete Anthology, Vol. 2* and *Reviews by Cat Ellington – The Complete Anthology Limited Edition Holiday Gift Set (Books 1 & 2)*, respectively.
And I must say that the experience has been nothing short of fabulous.

I thank all of you who have gone way beyond the call to support this series. Whether by way of a kind word spoken or otherwise. Thank you so much.

As I continue onward in my journey with this succession, I am honored to present *Reviews by Cat Ellington: The Complete Anthology, Vol. 3* for your reading pleasure.
Yet another great blessing bestowed upon me, book three represents my arrival into the digital age: Internet platforms, social media platforms, mobile applications, and, of course, eBooks. While the analyses in books 1 & 2 were written in an old-fashioned way—longhand—the thirty examinations that comprise this collection, though researched and noted manually, were all structured (digitally) on laptops and smart devices. It was a whole new animal, yes, but it was fun. And I quickly got the hang of it, even though there were many frustrating trials.

In my introduction, I will share some of the irritating roadblocks that I encountered along the route of my transfer to the Internet—where it pertains to my written analyses—and what I learned from many irreparable mistakes.

My dearest men and women, take a load off and enjoy yourselves. And I hope that all of you will enjoy reading this work as much as I did writing it.

Lovingly,

Cat Ellington

Acknowledgments

First and foremost—and always first and foremost—I humbly ascribe glory to my Lord and my God for all of His great gifts and blessings. For without Him, I could do nothing. And of this fact, I will forever be well aware. Praise be to the Father, the Son, and the Holy Spirit—the one and ONLY Divine Trinity.

Joe, thank you, baby. Thank you for providing your shoulder to me when I needed it to lean on. And thank you for all the wise words that you so generously shared with me over the many years that I've known you. I also thank you for your brilliant sense of humor: for you know how to make a gal bust-up in laughter. You are one of the best people. And I am so blessed to have you in my life. I love you as both my hubby and dearest friend.

Nathaniel, Nairobi, and Naras, I love you. Mama is so proud of all of you. And I am so honored to say that you three are the fruit of my womb, my groovy litter, my kiddens. And I love you always.

Freddie and Maurice, thank you, my beloved brothers, for all of your support, love, and encouragement. I am truly blessed to have both of you in my life. For ours is a beautiful fellowship.

John and the entire team at Google, thank you! You guys are the best—especially you, John. Thank you.

Thank you, team AUTHORSdb! Thank you so much.

As always, thank you to my readers.
Y'all stay groovy now, ya hear?

Love forever,

Cat Ellington

Introduction

Dear reader,

As *Reviews by Cat Ellington: The Complete Anthology, Vol. 3* marks the beginning of my foray into a brand new world of digitalization in literature, I thought that I would take the opportunity to shed a bit of light on my earlier experience with this new technology.

Before 2012, my entire library consisted of only print books in both hardcover and paperback formats. And I loved it. For over thirty years, I had only read physical books, and I loved it. I loved holding my books in hand and running my fingers over the glossy covers. I loved the habit of licking the tip of my index finger to turn every new page. I loved the "crisp" smell of the books (if the books were newly-purchased). I loved all of my stylish bookmarks, too. I loved the *feel* of the book's weight in my hand. And so on. I loved everything about the reading experience in the days of old. But once the so-called eReader—designed to carry massive digital libraries of so-called eBooks—came into being, that all changed.

While I admired this new form of technology, you know, the concept of reading electronic books on electronic devices, I'll admit that I had to get used to it. During the first couple of weeks, I kept tapping my tongue with the tip of my index finger to turn the pages, forgetting that the books were in a digital format and not printed. But that all soon subsided. Readers were also able to leave ratings and reviews at the end of each book, which I liked because the method allowed me to compose my (comprehensive) analyses by typing them onto my selected device rather than structuring them in longhand. The afforded convenience was addictive. And the entire process had been one smooth sail.

Indeed, everything had been going just fine until I decided to perform a factory reset on my old device. It was the same device on which I'd kept all of my reviews. They were in a folder in a reading app. But after the reset, they were gone - forever.

A factory reset restores a device to its original factory settings. And that was what I had wanted to do at the time. But what I failed to understand then is that I would have had to back up my files to protect them during the factory reset. And I did not do that. So in the wake of the restoration, I lost my reviews. And I cried for days about losing them. It hurt me that they were gone.

My book reviews I liken to my song works. And losing any of my examinations is the same to me as losing one of my song works.

The emotional pain that the loss of my reviews caused me was nothing short of anguishing. And trust, my dear reader, that I have never forgotten my error. For if truth be told, it was one of the biggest mistakes from which I have ever had to learn.

Structuring *Reviews by Cat Ellington: The Complete Anthology, Vol. 3* has been perhaps my most challenging effort yet because I had to start from scratch on any number of my critiques.

I had to rewrite some of the reviews (in this collection) from the pages of my handwritten notes. And for this reason, the original release date—April 2019—was pushed back until now.

While I am grateful to be done with this phase of my contribution, it is my profound hope that you will enjoy this collection and appreciate all of the hard work that it took to bring it to fruition.

Once again, I thank you for your interest in this, my respective contribution to the field of literature.

All my love,

Cat Ellington

Sketch of Cat Ellington by Joseph Strickland

January 1, 2013

Table of Contents

Chapter 1

Evolution in the New Era

Cat Ellington's review of Enemies and Playmates by Darcia Helle

My rating: 5 out of 5 stars

Date read: October, 2012

MEET ME AT THE BAR.

Everything is not as it seems.
Not even on the outstanding pages of this delectably romantic, albeit shamefully wicked, suspense thriller.

As the velvet curtain of its cover opens to introduce the reader to a talented ensemble—playing their parts in perfect unison with an expertly-crafted script—we make the acquaintance of our leading lady, Lauren Covington (a major in journalism at Harvard). Lauren is spending a night out on the town with her two best friends, the beautiful and ridiculously flirtatious Gina and Carrie, the techno-geek. It's a fun night out clubbing. And the three women, well, Gina and Carrie at least, are enjoying the atmosphere and all that it has to offer, including an ear-thumping sound system to which there is plenty of room to move on the massive dance floor. Not the socializing type outside of her circle, the shy Lauren, who has chosen to remain glued to the seat of her barstool, is sitting alone and watching her girls own the night. That is until Dean, the man seated on the barstool next to hers, leans over to drop a lame, drunken line – right before asking her out on a date. Of course, her answer is no - a very polite no.

Same old story. It's just another lonely evening out club-hopping with the besties. Lauren is practically bored to tears until she sees him across the room—ever so tall, confident, sexy, and solidly built—wearing a black leather jacket and loose-fitting jeans. Of all the women in the club, his piercing gaze is reserved only for Lauren Covington. And it's enough to make her blush.

Enter Jesse Ryder, a private investigator who just so happens to be in the employ of Lauren's godless father, Alex, a man she just so happens to hate with a passion. Jesse and Lauren have an inevitable mutual attraction. And they soon meet and greet over drinks at the bar. In time, Gina and Carrie join in the conversation, making pleasantries merry. And the evening is at peace with the crowd of four. But, determined not to be outdone, fate intervenes, urging the handsome Jesse to escort the timid Lauren to the dance floor, marking the beginning of a most fervently erotic love affair - and a most-vindictive rage.

LOOKS CAN BE DECEIVING.

The Covington family appear to have it all to those who peer into their affluent lives from the outside: unlimited money, a palatial home, only the finest of luxuries, a close-knit bond of unconditional love, and enviable respectability.

But it is all a lie.

It is all one hellish façade of a lie.

Physically, Alex Covington is a handsome, expensively-attired, upstanding, and phenomenally successful attorney at law. But spiritually, Alex Covington—this tale's hideously loathsome antagonist—is an individual prone to reprehensible evil.
A human host in the extremes of passive/aggressive dysfunction, Alex Covington nurtures only a few nauseating aspirations, one of which includes making everyday life a Hadean experience for his immediate family at home. Not one who fancies being challenged or contradicted, Alex Covington elects to enforce (and then reinforce) his alpha-male authority by way of both harsh words and violent action. And now aware of the romantic involvement between his only daughter and his archenemy *(that bastard, Jesse Ryder),* Alex Covington, clad in Armani, becomes the ultimate bringer of misery and destruction on all of those who dare to drift into his arrogant and unchaste orbit, including the young men intent on rebelling against his scandalous wishes: his son, Stephen Covington, and his intolerable employee, Jesse Ryder.

THE SUPPORT TEAM.

Rounding out a splendid, top-billed ensemble—who will remain imprinted on the reader's psyche long after the final page unfurls—are the following:

- Kara Covington, who stuns as a desperate wife and a mother beaten into submission

- Suzanne Sampson, a blonde bombshell and faithful secretary to Alex Covington

- Chris Nyles, a convicted murderer and former associate of Alex Covington

- Tim O'Leary, best friend to Jesse Ryder and fellow hard-nosed detective hot on the heels of depraved criminality

These are all offset by only a small troupe of supporting and bit players, including:

- Kevin Fuller, the good-looking, badass friend of Stephen Covington and candyman to the rich and bored

- Paul Stosh, Lauren's empathetic boss

- Captain James Barnes, a mutual acquaintance of Alex Covington and officer on the take

- Marc Wilkes, a true guardian angel if there were ever one

FLATTERING WORDS.

Striking one conniving blow after another, the Boston-based *Enemies and Playmates* is a fictional time bomb recommended for every fan of romantic thrillers. Darcia Helle gives it her very best with this novel. And I am beyond honored to have received a complimentary copy. What an exceptional effort, Darcia Helle!

Five tyrannical stars.

Cat Ellington's review of Heller (Heller, #1) by J.D. Nixon

My rating: 5 out of 5 stars

Date read: October, 2012

A QUIET GEM.

I first read *Heller* (*Heller, #1*) via the *Kindle* app on my smartphone in October of 2012 - which was nearly a year after the novel's release. And although I'd composed a more detailed review of the work in the wake of completing it, I still cannot find my original review. Therefore, I have concluded that I had perhaps stored it away with a small batch of other reviews missing from my collection in my second city of residence. That or the examination is lost forever.

Regardless of whatever the case may be, I am inclined to render this exciting action thriller the genuine praise - of which it is well-deserving.

In brief, *Heller* (*Heller, #1*) is a memorable tale starring Matilda "Tilly" Chalmers. Tilly plays a young security specialist who is way up the industry ladder to obtain a successful career in her field of expertise at Heller's Security & Surveillance. But as Tilly gets comfortable in her new job, chaos arrives to test her to the furthest limit.

Heller (*Heller, #1*) is a beautiful dialogue seeped in romantic undertones between Tilly and her powerful and no-nonsense boss, Mr. Heller, vengeance, deception, lies, and cold-blooded murder.

A charming and cozy narrative that I am sure many action thriller fans will enjoy immensely, *Heller* (*Heller, #1*) is a quietly precious gem worthy of not only a lazy afternoon read but also my loftiest ranking.
Great work, J.D. Nixon.

Five armed-and-totally-dangerous stars.

Cat Ellington's review of Deadly Offerings (Deadly Trilogy, #1) by Alexa Grace

My rating: 4 out of 5 stars

Date read: October, 2012

STALKED BY A KILLER.

Much like J.D. Nixon's *Heller* (*Heller, #1*), *Deadly Offerings* (*Deadly Trilogy, #1*) had been yet another effort in my brand new library of eBooks that I'd completed during the earlier days of my delve into the Internet sphere. It was October of 2012, to be exact, that I'd received this fictional work free of charge via *Barnes & Noble*. And immediately taken by the title's description, I dove—headfirst—into the plot, soon falling madly in love with its gorgeous leading lady, Anne Mason, as well as with its fast-paced suspense and its intriguing mystery.

Deadly Offerings (*Deadly Trilogy, #1*) is a good book that I enjoyed reading back in 2012. Unfortunately, though, I lost the original review in the factory reset I spoke about earlier. On these gripping pages, the plot orbits around a psychotic murderer who hunts and kills his victims before discarding their remains in a cornfield. The cornfield is on a farm owned by Anne. And the killer aims to send her a morbid message that she will soon be among the dead.

While it is unfortunate that I cannot locate the small collection of analyses; nevertheless, I had to honor this fascinating psychological thriller with a critique of which it is tremendously worthy - even if it is brief.

OH, AND ANOTHER THING:

Although our leading man, Michael Brandt, annoyed me beyond what is tolerable—due to the extremities of his possessive nature towards the auburn-haired Anne—*Deadly Offerings* (*Deadly Trilogy, #1*) kept my reader enticed and thoroughly entertained from beginning to end. Aside from Michael Brandt's nettlesome actions, the narrative is splendid in ensemble and structure. And I will always be willing to add a little more wind to its stunning sails.

As an afterthought, I should perhaps add that there is no such thing as anyone being loved too much by someone else. Especially not if that person just so happens to be his or her significant other - as is the case with Michael Brandt and Anne Mason, respectively. But his performance on these pages is just a breath away from an obsessive-compulsive disorder where it concerns Anne. And for no reason other than his irritating behavior, this work has been robbed of a five-star rating.

Happy reading, all.

Cat Ellington's review of Big Girls Don't Cry by Gretchen Lane

My rating: 5 out of 5 stars

Date read: October, 2012

A WHOLE LOTTA LOVELINESS.

A few pounds overweight or not, aspiring model Gretchen Lane can be one atrociously sexy woman if only she puts her mind to it. But in the constant crosshairs of bitter scorn, malicious mockeries, and spiteful ridicule from others—strangers at that—bonding with self-esteem can be downright impossible.

Gretchen Lane is an obese twenty-four-year-old virgin who spends her days working an average job, chatting on the phone with her best friend, Michelle, and, quite naturally, eating. And until now, she has become conditioned in the flesh of her bulky weight, hiding out in her home and relieving her sexual tensions by way of erotic fantasies and a bedside pleasure chest.

Gretchen Lane is not unlike the typical fat girl, meaning a standard target of cruel and hateful mistreatment. It's the story of her life. And, unfortunately, Gretchen has grown more accustomed to it. That isn't to say she enjoys it, only that she has come to expect it. However, it isn't until after she gets assaulted by someone who throws a 32-ounce soft drink at her that she begins to realize that there has to be more to her life than this, what being called horrible names and having someone smack her in the face with a large cup filled with frigid ice and pop. There has to be more to life than that. Gretchen Lane knows this. And soon enough, she decides to do something about it. She'll hire herself a personal trainer. And together, they'll tackle her antagonistic weight down to size.

A personal trainer. She, Gretchen Lane, of all chubby gals, will have her very own personal trainer. Oh, it's going to be so exciting!

And how.

If only she knew that her future personal trainer would be the provocative, rough, and rugged Billy Mack. The buffed extraordinaire.

DON'T MESS WITH BILL.

Chubby or not, Gretchen Lane is beautiful in the eyes of her beholder, Billy Mack. And as their new friendship blossoms and grows into something more dramatically adult-themed, Billy, the man of Gretchen's erotic dreams, takes the passionate initiative, unwrapping her to reveal that special gift of man-eating love.

And boy, does he love her.

SPITFIRE AND DESIRE.

I must say that I, too, fell madly in love with Gretchen Lane throughout this short-lived tale of heat-inducing erotica—as she is perfection.

Gretchen and Billy's newfound romance is deep, wild, sweaty, and heart-pounding. And as they romp about in the intense fire of their burning desire, Gretchen will soon learn that Billy Mack's loins are not his only fierce attribute: for a rival to his (blessed) manhood is his explosive temper. Indeed, it must be that offenses come, but woe to that man by whom the offense comes, especially when Billy Mack's new girlfriend, the tubby Gretchen Lane, is the target thereof.

A REVIEWER SMITTEN.

For a work of erotic fiction with pagination of only 57, *Big Girls Don't Cry* packs a powerful punch from start to finish. And I can't imagine any pundit of the erotica genre not admiring its script and the applause-worthy performances of its memorable cast as much as I did.

Big Girls Don't Cry, a great read, indeed, was my introduction to the alluring literature of its fascinating authorship, Gretchen Lane. And it is with genuine anticipation that I look forward to making the acquaintance *Big Girls Don't Cry 2: The Emancipation of Gretchen*, its successor in the series.
My fellow reader, I highly recommend this effort for your reading pleasure. But please note that the storyline contains erotica, including anal penetration, and therefore must be approached with caution—should you be of those given to discomfort by such explicitly graphic content.

Five erect-and-lubricated stars.

Thank you for reading.

www.ingramcontent.com/pod-product-compliance
Lightning Source LLC
Chambersburg PA
CBHW021155020426
42331CB00003B/72